The Open University

SCIENCE MATTERS

Biological Conservation

prepared for the Course Team by Michael Gillman

Science: a second level course

The S280 Course Team

Pam Berry (Text Processing)

Norman Cohen (Author)

Angela Colling (Author)

Michael Gillman (Author)

John Greenwood (Librarian)

Barbara Hodgson (Reader)

David Johnson (Author)

Carol Johnstone (Course Secretary)

Hilary MacQueen (Author)

Isla McTaggart (Course Manager)

Diane Mole (Designer)

Joanna Munnelly (Editor)

Pat Murphy (Author)

Ian Nuttall (Editor)

Pam Owen (Graphic Artist)

Malcolm Scott (Author)

Sandy Smith (Author)

Margaret Swithenby (Editor)

Jeff Thomas (Course Team Chair and Author)

Kiki Warr (Author)

Bill Young (BBC Producer)

External Assessor: John Durant

The Open University, Walton Hall, Milton Keynes, MK7 6AA.

First published 1993.

Edited, designed and typeset in the United Kingdom by the Open University.

Printed in the United Kingdom by Eyre & Spottiswoode Ltd, Margate, Kent.

ISBN 0749251026

This text forms part of an Open University Second Level Course. If you have not enrolled on the course and would like to buy this or other Open University material, please write to Open University Educational Enterprises Ltd, 12 Cofferidge Close, Stony Stratford, Milton Keynes, MK11 1BY, United Kingdom. If you would like a copy of *Studying with the Open University*, please write to the Central Enquiry Office, PO Box 200, The Open University, Walton Hall, Milton Keynes, MK7 6YZ, United Kingdom

1.1

5898C/s280BiCon

Contents

1 Raising awareness

Biological conservation is an important and complex subject, in which science should play a key role in identifying problems and seeking solutions. The variety, complexity and international nature of conservation *problems* can be seen in the selection of examples presented in Figure 1.1; Figure 1.2 describes a range of appropriate *responses* to the types of problem identified in Figure 1.1. All the extracts in these figures are taken from the introductory paragraphs of articles published in the weekly popular science journal *New Scientist*. The following activity asks you to draw points of wider relevance from these few examples, in anticipation of more detailed discussion in later chapters.

Activity 1.1   *You should spend up to 20 minutes on this activity.*

Read the extracts in Figure 1.1 carefully. To prompt you to think more about the underlying causes of the problems, answer questions (a)–(d).

(a) Which problems arise directly or indirectly from human influences?

Now attempt to *classify* these problems more precisely. (Use the information in the answer to (a) where appropriate.)

(b) Which are caused by the direct exploitation of animals or plants?

(c) Which arise from the use of habitats by humans for recreation?

(d) Which arise from the indirect impact of human activities, e.g. agriculture, pollution?

Answering these questions should have prompted you to think more about the *reasons* for our present day concerns with conservation. Also, you have classified a range of particular problems into broad categories that describe general issues of conservation. As you know, the processes of classification and of generalizing from particular examples are both of fundamental importance in science.

Now consider the responses shown in Figure 1.2. They indicate some of the approaches adopted, and some of the difficulties that arise as conservation problems are tackled. Once again, you should aim to draw out issues of general importance to conservation from these few examples.

(e) What general strategies for the preservation of endangered animals or plants are described in the extracts?

(f) Provide one example where commercial interests and conservation policies are (i) in conflict, and (ii) seemingly acting together.

(g) Provide one example where 'direct action' is needed to ensure habitat preservation.

(h) In your opinion, which two extracts best illustrate the fact that effective conservation policies depend critically on precise scientific information about species and their vulnerability.

A number of general points emerge from Activity 1.1 that will provide a focus for much of the book. First, conservation reflects a desire to avoid the loss of *species* and *habitats*—as Chapter 2 shows, the two are inextricably linked. However, this raises an awkward and fundamental question: why should conservation be regarded as desir-

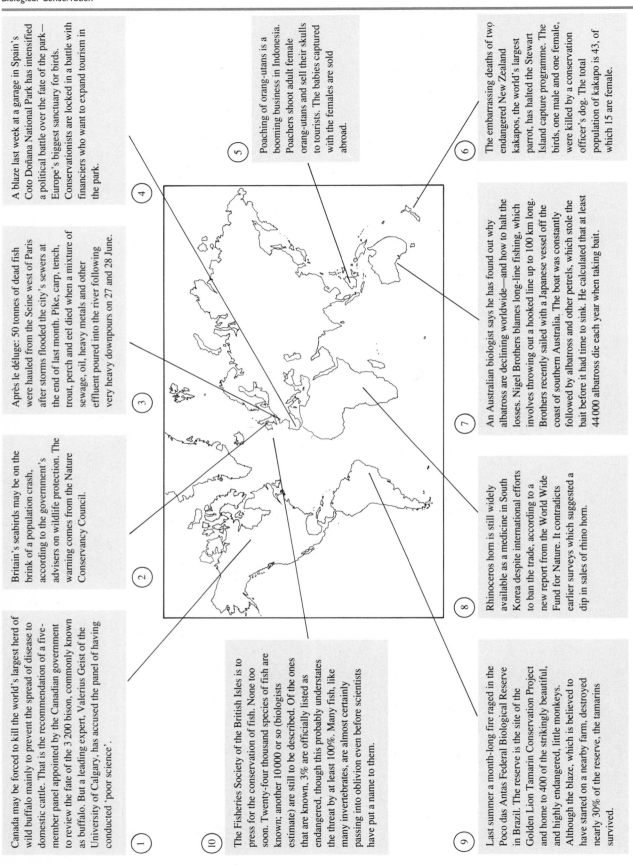

1. Canada may be forced to kill the world's largest herd of wild buffalo mainly to prevent the spread of disease to domestic cattle. That is the recommendation of a five-member panel appointed by the Canadian government to review the fate of the 3 200 bison, commonly known as buffalo. But a leading expert, Valerius Geist of the University of Calgary, has accused the panel of having conducted 'poor science'.

2. Britain's seabirds may be on the brink of a population crash, according to the government's advisers on wildlife protection. The warning comes from the Nature Conservancy Council.

3. Après le déluge: 50 tonnes of dead fish were hauled from the Seine west of Paris after storms flooded the city's sewers at the end of last month. Pike, carp, tench, trout, perch and eel died when a mixture of sewage, oil, heavy metals and other effluent poured into the river following very heavy downpours on 27 and 28 June.

4. A blaze last week at a garage in Spain's Coto Doñana National Park has intensified a political battle over the fate of the park—Europe's biggest sanctuary for birds. Conservationists are locked in a battle with financiers who want to expand tourism in the park.

5. Poaching of orang-utans is a booming business in Indonesia. Poachers shoot adult female orang-utans and sell their skulls to tourists. The babies captured with the females are sold abroad.

6. The embarrassing deaths of two endangered New Zealand kakapos, the world's largest parrot, has halted the Stewart Island capture programme. The birds, one male and one female, were killed by a conservation officer's dog. The total population of kakapo is 43, of which 15 are female.

7. An Australian biologist says he has found out why albatross are declining worldwide—and how to halt the losses. Nigel Brothers blames long-line fishing, which involves throwing out a hooked line up to 100 km long. Brothers recently sailed with a Japanese vessel off the coast of southern Australia. The boat was constantly followed by albatross and other petrels, which stole the bait before it had time to sink. He calculated that at least 44000 albatross die each year when taking bait.

8. Rhinoceros horn is still widely available as a medicine in South Korea despite international efforts to ban the trade, according to a new report from the World Wide Fund for Nature. It contradicts earlier surveys which suggested a dip in sales of rhino horn.

9. Last summer a month-long fire raged in the Poço das Antas Federal Biological Reserve in Brazil. The reserve is the site of the Golden Lion Tamarin Conservation Project and home to 400 of the strikingly beautiful, and highly endangered, little monkeys. Although the blaze, which is believed to have started on a nearby farm, destroyed nearly 30% of the reserve, the tamarins survived.

10. The Fisheries Society of the British Isles is to press for the conservation of fish. None too soon. Twenty-four thousand species of fish are known; another 10000 or so (biologists estimate) are still to be described. Of the ones that are known, 3% are officially listed as endangered, though this probably understates the threat by at least 100%. Many fish, like many invertebrates, are almost certainly passing into oblivion even before scientists have put a name to them.

Figure 1.1 A selection of global conservation problems. The extracts were from the following issues of *New Scientist* in 1990: 7 April (4), 14 April (8), 14 July (3), 11 August (10), 15 September (1, 6), 29 September (7), 1 December (2), 8 December (5), 15 December (9).

4 An extinct bird has been turning up on the dinner plates of Vietnamese farmers. The Vietnamese pheasant, discovered only 25 years ago, was thought to be extinct until ornithologists optimistically searching for any remaining specimens found a group of hunters who said they regularly trapped and ate the bird.

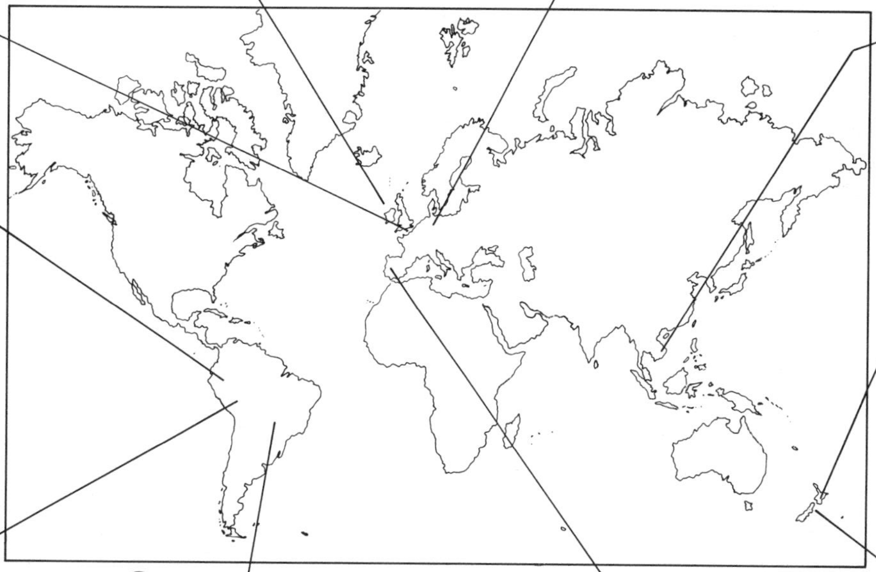

5 A campaign to stop possums destroying one of the world's rarest native forests began this week in Northland, the northernmost part of New Zealand, with an airdrop of 100 tonnes of poisonous bran pellets. Officials hope the pellets will exterminate the possum (*Trichosurus vulpecula*). In 1858, some 300 possums were introduced to New Zealand from its native Australia, where it is now a protected species. Their population has since risen to 70 million. Ironically, campaigners protesting against possum fur coats have helped the population explosion by depressing international trading in possum fur.

6 When a 9-year-old parrot called Heather laid an egg in February, she became an international celebrity. Her story was broadcast on New Zealand's morning news, and reached newspapers and magazines around the world. The reason for Heather's overnight fame is that she is a kakapo, one of perhaps only 43 that survive. Her egg was a sign that her species may have won a reprieve at last.

3 Thanks to five families of sea eagles nesting in the 'death strip', once the border between East and West Germany, some East German border police have yet to drop their binoculars and abandon the watchtowers. The thriving ecosystem that has developed in the zone needs protection. A single sea eagle egg can fetch between £2000 and £7000 from collectors. A few nests have already been ransacked. So, instead of keeping people in East Germany, the border police have been asked to keep the sea eagle eggs in their nests.

2 All dolphins and porpoises stranded around Britain's coasts are to be tested for pollutants such as polychlorinated biphenyls and DDT, as part of research projects on marine animals costing £500 000 announced by the Department of the Environment last week.

7 Eleven young red kites, imported from Spain earlier this year, were released from a secret location in Britain last week in a bid to re-establish the endangered species in England and Scotland after a century-long absence. A similar exercise was carried out last year but two of the eleven birds released were poisoned. The population in Wales is in a healthier state.

8 The Brazilian government is embroiled in a row with ecologists over plans to allow captive breeding of wild animals purely for commercial purposes. So far it has given the go-ahead for private breeders to 'ranch' alligators, snakes and large rodents called capybaras. The government claims that this is a way of protecting the animals from extinction, much to the disgust of conservation groups.

1 This is the equivalent of a five-star hotel, if you happen to be a Celebes black macaque. The Universities Federation for Animal Welfare last week awarded Jersey Zoo a prize for the enclosure, which supports 20 macaques. Roger Ewbank, director of the federation, said: 'It fulfils three main objectives: conservation, animal welfare and education... The actual welfare of the animals is improved by having plenty of landscaped space, reflecting that found in the wild, to enrich their lives.'

10 Two American companies are hoping that their customers will pay a little extra for shirts and jackets adorned with buttons from the tropical rainforest. They have agreed to buy a million buttons made from the tagua nut, which grows on palm trees in the Ecuadorian rainforest. Buttons made from tagua look like ivory, and were widely used before cheap plastic buttons drove them from the world market in the 1930s. Conservation International, an environmental group, has persuaded the companies that products from the rainforest will generate good publicity and sales. The group believes the rainforest will be better protected if local communities make a better living from its natural products.

9 The ecology-conscious government of the Netherlands is considering a plan to offset emissions from Dutch power stations by replanting the rainforests of South America. The plan, first suggested by environmentalists from Utrecht University, has been developed by the Netherlands' Electricity Generating Board (SEP) in consultation with the Ministries of Environment and Agriculture. It involves replanting over 25 years some 250 000 hectares of tropical rainforest burnt or cut down in Bolivia, Peru, Colombia, Ecuador and Costa Rica. Brazil is excluded because of what the Dutch describe as its 'poor reforestation programme'.

Figure 1.2 A selection of possible responses to global conservation problems. The extracts were from the following issues of *New Scientist* in 1990: 21 April (9), 16 June (6), 23 June (5), 14 July (2), 21 July (1, 7), 4 August (3), 15 September (10), 20 October (8), 8 December (4).

able? This key issue is addressed in Chapter 3. Defining a problem and devising an appropriate response requires precise information, which is why *monitoring* the abundance and distribution of species is a vital element in modern biological conservation, as Chapter 4 demonstrates. The variety of 'direct actions', described in Figure 1.2, shows that conservation involves much more than a simple preservation of the status quo: Chapter 5 illustrates that it requires active interference, more properly termed *management*. Finally, Chapter 6 reveals how we need to look at the complete range of plant and animal species—the *biological diversity* of the Earth—in order to understand fully the key problems of conservation and to determine our responses.

This book is therefore concerned with how scientific understanding can help identify and quantify problems of biological conservation and suggest possible responses. We shall see that 'responses' such as species protection, monitoring and management bring their own problems. In this area, as with so many others where scientific understanding plays a key role, there are rarely simple, clear-cut answers, especially because science invariably becomes entangled with 'social' issues such as ethics, economics and our continuing exploitation of the environment.

(a)

(b)

Plate 2.1 An example of habitat monitoring by remote sensing. Satellite images of the vegetation and physical features around Brighton in East Sussex (a), and Malham in North Yorkshire (b). The false colour image of Brighton and district was taken in April, and shows urban areas (royal blue to blue–grey), vigorously growing vegetation such as oilseed rape (red), slow-growing vegetation such as unfertilized grassland (orange), and the English Channel (blue–black). The false colour image of Malham was taken in late May, and shows hay meadows in the bottoms of the dales (orange), unfertilized hill grassland (pale blue to green), and conifer plantations (dark brown blocks). Each image is about 25 km across.

Plate 2.2 An example of species and habitat monitoring. Recording the number of plants in a fixed area of grassland.

(a)   (b)   (c)

Plate 3.1 Three species of orchid. There are approximately 18 000 species of orchid and 750–800 genera, many of which are tropical. All of the species shown here are found in Britain and mainland Europe. (a) Lady's slipper orchid (*Cypripedium calceolus* L.). (b) Dark red helleborine (*Epipactis atrorubens*). (c) Marsh orchid (*Dactylorhiza* sp., where sp. indicates one of several very similar species of *Dactylorhiza*).

Plate 3.2   An example of a butterfly mimicry complex. These butterfly species all live in the same area, and show either Batesian or Müllerian mimicry.

Plate 4.1   The early spider orchid (*Ophrys sphegodes*). Non-flowering plants form small rosettes which may only occupy an area of 1 cm^2.

(a)

(b)

Plate 5.1   A comparison between a quarry left for more than 20 years after the end of working (a) and one from which rock is currently being extracted (b). The two photographs were taken from the same point, turning through 180°.

Plate 5.2 A selection of plants that increased and decreased in number after the decline in grazing of chalk grassland. (a) Hawthorn (*Crataegus monogyna*), (b) deadly nightshade (*Atropa belladonna*), and (c) ragwort (*Senecio jacobaea*).

(a)

(b)

(c)

2 The nature of biological conservation

As the variety and breadth of the examples in Figures 1.1 and 1.2 imply, biological conservation is a subject that is difficult to delimit or define. The purpose of this chapter is to examine in more depth what the term implies, and work towards a broad definition of the subject. Our approach here will be to build upon the discussion of 'problems' and 'responses' in Chapter 1 and to introduce key ideas related to biological conservation that will be explored in greater detail in later chapters.

We start by highlighting what may strike you as a rather negative aspect—the present day losses of the world's species and habitats. But this is a sensible place to start because there would be no need for biological conservation (and this book!) if exceptional levels of species extinction and habitat loss were not now in evidence. Before we begin to explore these phenomena it is important to understand the meaning of the terms 'species' and 'habitat', and their relationship to each other.

2.1 Plants, animals and their habitats

2.1.1 Defining species and habitat

Various observable differences allow animals and plants to be put into named categories, such as elephant, giraffe or oak tree. On closer inspection these categories can be seen to be divisible into a series of smaller categories; for example, there are at least two types of elephant (the African and the Asian, Figure 2.1) distinguishable by their size (the African is larger) and various other characteristics, such as their teeth and the size of their ears.

African elephants can be further divided into three separate types, based on size and habitat preferences: the forest or round-eared, the bush or large-eared, and the pygmy. Consider another example: there are two types of deciduous oak tree in Britain, distinguishable by, amongst other things, the length of the stalk attached to the acorn

Figure 2.1 The African and Asian elephants.

African elephant

Asian elephant

(called the peduncle, Figure 2.2). In both examples, structural features are used to assign organisms to particular types. There may also be less obvious, though very significant, differences in characteristics, such as biochemical composition, that enable us to distinguish between different types.

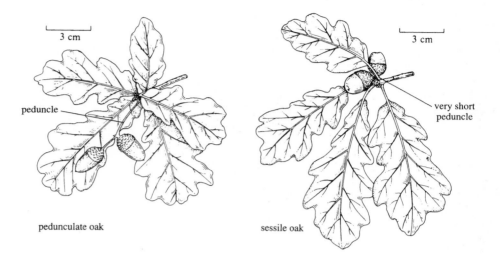

Figure 2.2 The peduncle of the pedunculate oak, compared with the sessile oak.

That two individuals possess different characteristics does not necessarily mean that they belong to different species. A **species** is defined strictly as comprising all organisms which are able to interbreed and produce viable (healthy and fertile) offspring. Two closely related species may be able to produce hybrids, but these should be infertile. Where individuals *appear* to comprise different species, based on certain characteristics, but in fact are able to interbreed, they may be referred to as subspecies. These subspecies may, over time, evolve to become separate species.

▷   The elephants in Africa may be of different sizes in different parts of the continent but they all (at least those of the opposite sex) have the *potential* to interbreed and produce fertile offspring. Are they therefore all the same species?

▶   Yes.

▷   The African and Asian elephants are *un*able to interbreed and produce fertile offspring. Do they therefore constitute different species?

▶   Yes.

▷   What is a suitable description for the forest and bush (African) elephants?

▶   They can be considered as different *sub*species, but part of the same species of African elephant.

It is important to realize that it is often not possible to apply the 'interbreeding test' to decide if two individuals are from the same species. For example, it is difficult to apply the test to fossil organisms! Even for most living organisms, species are distinguished primarily on the basis of structural characteristics, such as the oak peduncle in Figure 2.2. If the interbreeding test is unavailable, it is possible to lump together wrongly two true species into one and, conversely, to split a true species into two.

Box 2.1 Naming species

It is conventional to give species a **scientific name** in Latin. This is in addition to the organism's common name. The name 'oak' is a common name, derived from the Anglo-Saxon 'ac' meaning fruit or acorn. The common name, the pedunculate oak (Figure 2.2), is in fact quite a good one because it identifies an important characteristic of this species. Unfortunately, it has a second common name—the common oak! Conversely, one common name may correspond to several species. Therefore, to avoid confusion and ensure that each species has one name which is used internationally, the common or pedunculate oak also has the scientific name *Quercus robur*. The system of having a general name (*Quercus* is the **genus**, plural **genera**) followed by a specific name (*robur* is the species) was introduced by the Swedish botanist Carolus Linnaeus (1707–1778). Furthermore, Linnaeus was also the first person to give the pedunculate oak the name *Quercus robur*. This fact is signified by putting his initial after the name. So, the full scientific name is *Quercus robur* L.

Incidentally, the origins of the two parts of this scientific name are quite obscure. *Quercus* is an old Latin name which is used for all oak species. To confuse matters it is possibly associated with the Greek for pig, *choiros*, because pigs are fond of acorns! The species name *robur* apparently means 'strength' or possibly 'hardwood' or 'elite', all suitable names for the oak.

▷ What is the scientific name that indicates that a tree species is an oak?

▶ All oak trees have the name *Quercus*. This is referred to as the genus, meaning the general name for oaks. ■

Question 2.1 Identify the species, genus and common names in the following: human (*Homo sapiens*) and lady's slipper orchid (*Cypripedium calceolus*).

In this book, we follow the practice of giving both the scientific and the common names of the individual plants and animals mentioned. This is done for completeness; you are not expected to remember the scientific names which, as you will see, is just as well, given their indigestibility.

A **population** is a group of individuals of the same species and is usually a spatially discrete entity. In other words, all the individuals of a population live close to each other and are therefore potentially able to mate with each other. Individuals from different populations, although of the same species, are less likely to mate. A subspecies may comprise a single population.

A **habitat** is defined as the type of environment where individuals of a species live. These habitats may occur in salt or freshwater or on land (terrestrial). This book deals mainly with terrestrial habitats, although it will occasionally be necessary to draw on aquatic examples. Some species are restricted to a single type of habitat or a very narrow set of habitats, whilst others may occur over a wide range. Habitats are defined at different spatial scales so that one broad habitat category may contain a number of sub- or micro-habitats (Section 2.1.2). In the following example we consider the factors which determine categories of terrestrial habitat at the largest spatial scale.

2.1.2 Examples of species and habitats in Australia

Australia has a wide range of habitat types and associated species, many of which are unique to that continent. The four broad categories of terrestrial Australian habitat shown in Figure 2.3 are defined with respect to their major vegetation (plant) types. Thus these areas of land may be dominated by trees (forest or woodland), bushes/small trees (scrub), grasses (grassland), or desert vegetation.

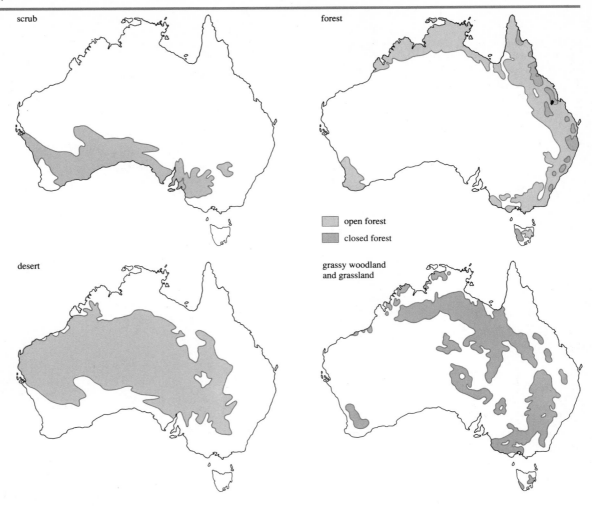

scrub

forest

open forest

closed forest

desert

grassy woodland
and grassland

Figure 2.3 The distribution of four categories of habitat in Australia (desert, scrub, grassy woodland, grassland and open and closed forest). The distinction in this figure between closed and open forest is determined by the spacing of trees. Similarly, 'woodland' is defined as more open than 'open forest'. This particular distinction between woodland and forest is not always applied in other regions of the world.

Each of the Australian habitat types in Figure 2.3, apart from being dominated or characterized by particular types of vegetation, also contains plant or animal species peculiar to it. Some examples of species associated with two of these habitats are given in Figure 2.4.

The eucalyptus trees are one of the most famous group of Australian plant species. In fact *Eucalyptus* is a genus with approximately 450 species comprising an important natural component of the Australian forest and woodland. The koala 'bear' (*Phascolarctos cinereus*), which is really a marsupial, is a species restricted to forest habitats because it primarily eats the *Eucalyptus* leaves found in these forests. Indeed, the koala, like many other Australian plants and animals, is restricted to Australia. The entire **geographical range** of the koala is therefore contained within the forested areas of eastern Australia. The reason why Australasia has such an unusual and restricted flora and fauna can be explained by continental drift, and the continent's relatively long period of isolation.

Two common grass species (not shown in Figure 2.4) have names which indicate the animals with which they share their habitat: kangaroo grass (*Themeda australis*) and common wallaby grass (*Danthonia caespitosa*) are dominant over large areas of grassland (common wallaby grass especially in the south). Most kangaroo and wallaby species are herbivorous and it is the feeding by such species that is partly responsible for maintaining the grassland habitat, just as a lawn-mower maintains a lawn. Grasses do well under grazing or lawn-mowing because they have growing points (meristems)

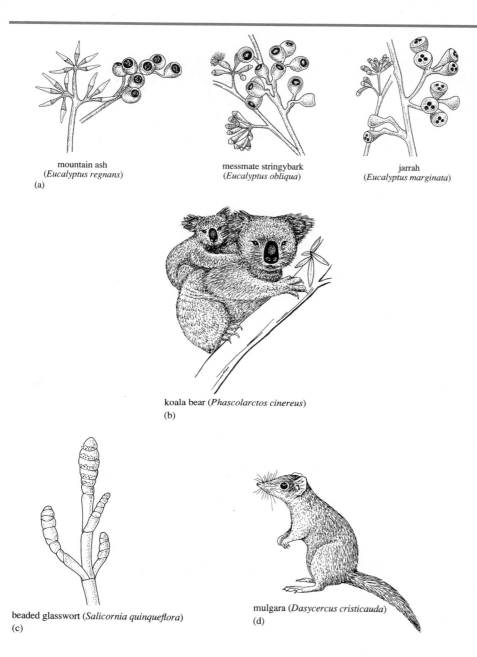

mountain ash
(*Eucalyptus regnans*)
(a)

messmate stringybark
(*Eucalyptus obliqua*)

jarrah
(*Eucalyptus marginata*)

Eucalyptus sp.

koala bear (*Phascolarctos cinereus*)
(b)

beaded glasswort (*Salicornia quinqueflora*)
(c)

mulgara (*Dasycercus cristicauda*)
(d)

Figure 2.4 Species associated with two of the Australian habitats in Figure 2.3 — (not drawn to scale). Forest species include (a) *Eucalyptus* species (a genus of trees native to Australia, but widely planted in other tropical regions such as India, that can reach heights of up to 50–60 metres), and (b) the koala bear (*Phascolarctos cinereus*). (c) The beaded glasswort (*Salicornia quinqueflora*) is a desert plant species. Note the fleshy leaves which are characteristic of species living in very dry conditions. (d) The mulgara (*Dasycercus cristicauda*) is found in dry stony desert where it feeds on insects, small mammals and reptiles, and is able to survive without drinking by extracting water from its prey.

close to the ground away from the teeth of grazing animals such as sheep and kangeroos. Thus grasses can survive being eaten whilst other species, such as young tree seedlings, which have meristems at the apex or tip of their stem, may be killed by grazing. If herbivores are removed then, in many areas, trees will eventually dominate the landscape. The same might happen if you left your lawn uncut for 50 years!

The distribution of vegetation types, such as that shown in Figure 2.3, often corresponds quite well to patterns of climatic variables, particularly rainfall and temperature. Figure 2.5 shows the patterns of annual rainfall and July temperatures for Australia.

▷ What are the most obvious relationships revealed by comparing Figures 2.3 and 2.5a?

▶ The desert in Figure 2.3 clearly corresponds to the area of lowest rainfall, whilst the closed and open forests occur in areas of highest rainfall.

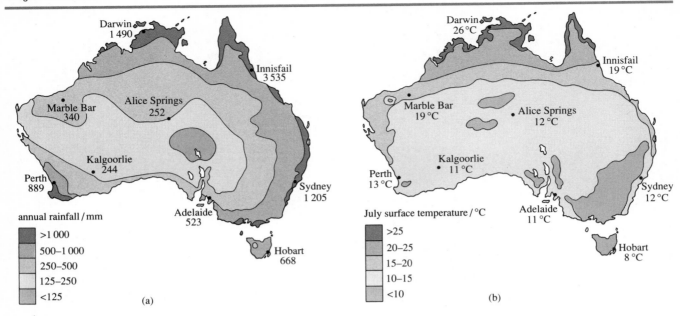

annual rainfall / mm

- >1 000
- 500–1 000
- 250–500
- 125–250
- <125

(a)

July surface temperature / °C

- >25
- 20–25
- 15–20
- 10–15
- <10

(b)

Figure 2.5 Patterns of (a) mean annual rainfall (mm), and (b) mean July surface temperature (°C) in Australia.

The distribution of grassy woodland, grassland and scrub do not appear to relate so closely to the patterns in Figure 2.5. There are two reasons for this. First, the *annual* rainfall pattern gives a misleading picture (except at the extremes of very low or very high rainfall): during Australian summers the rainfall is highest in the north and north-west of the country, whilst in winter it is highest in the southern tips and south-east of the country. Secondly, the pattern of dominant vegetation is often influenced by soil type as well as climate, and so relates to surface geology.

2.1.3 The relationship between habitat and climate

Despite the difficulties of interpretation, the relationship between climate and broad habitat type (defined with respect to the dominant vegetation) is sufficiently robust to allow the production of a convincing graph showing the types of world habitat in relation to rainfall and temperature (Figure 2.6). Most of the habitat types in Figure 2.6 should be familiar to you. **Tropical moist forest** is a collective term used for a range of tropical forest types; tropical rainforest is included within this category, occurring at the wetter end of the scale, together with tropical seasonal forest at the drier end of the scale.

Question 2.2 Based on Figure 2.6:

(a) what is unusual about the way the scale on the vertical axis of the graph is represented?

(b) at a mean temperature of 25 °C, what is the effect of an increase in precipitation from 1 000 to 3 500 mm per year?

The discussion so far has led to a general categorization of habitats according to climatic variables; these habitat categories, called **biomes**, refer to the main vegetation types and are shown in Figure 2.6. The distribution of animal species is then determined by these biomes. We can therefore define a sequence of factors which determine habitat; *climate* determines *biome*, which in turn determines the *animal species* present. Complications to this simple scheme arise because animals may modify a habitat that is

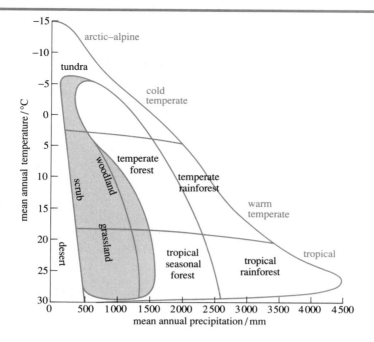

Figure 2.6 The various world habitat types (biomes) arranged according to mean annual precipitation (rainfall) and mean annual temperature. The effects of soil type and fire can change the vegetation between woodland and grassland in the shaded region of the graph. General climatic zones are labelled in green: Britain is à typical temperate region. Note that the term tropical moist forest is sometimes used as the collective term for tropical rainforest and tropical seasonal forest.

initially plant-determined. Also, the biome categories may be subdivided, for example, according to different soil types. Despite these complications, the idea of climate determining types of plant habitat which then determine animal distribution works well enough as a first approximation.

Smaller subdivisions of habitat may occur if one considers particular individuals within the habitat. A tree of a certain species (which may be one of many tree species in a woodland habitat) may be home to a particular species of herbivorous insect, i.e. the tree constitutes a habitat for that insect species. Similarly, that (herbivorous) insect may in turn be the habitat for a particular species of parasitic insect living in or on it.

2.2 The link between habitat loss and species extinction

Species extinction means the complete loss of a species.

▷ Which two factors may be responsible for the extinction of a species?

▶ Loss of the place where the species lives (its habitat) and thus its food source, or direct reduction of its numbers, e.g. by hunting or disease.

If a species is restricted to one particular habitat and that habitat is reduced in size, then this clearly increases the likelihood of species extinction. The extreme case would be the complete loss of a habitat. Complete loss of, for example, *Eucalyptus* forest would result in extinction of the koala (because of the loss of its food source), along with many thousands of other species. Even partial loss or degradation of a habitat may result in the demise of a species, perhaps in combination with hunting. The koala (Figure 2.4) provides a poignant example of the impact of hunting. The koala is the model 'cuddly teddy bear'. In spite of, or because of, this fact, millions of these animals were shot in the 1920s, resulting in the near extinction of the species.

In 1924, two million skins were exported from Australia, leaving the species close to extinction in New South Wales, Victoria and South Australia. In Chapter 3 we examine other cases where hunting, rather than habitat loss, is the most important factor determining the decline of the species.

In the next section, we consider an example of the loss of a particular habitat and the effect on species extinction.

2.2.1 Tropical moist forest

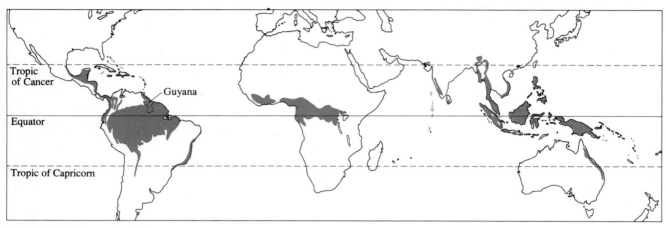

Figure 2.7 The world distribution of tropical moist forest.

It is often said of tropical moist forests (Figure 2.7) that they are the most 'species-rich' habitats in the world. World-wide, it is estimated that about one-half of *all* known species are found in tropical moist forests. We are only now beginning to learn about the extraordinary number of different species in these forests—particularly insect species (a subject which will be covered in Chapter 6). Some insect groups have been quite well studied in the tropics and give us an idea of the total richness of insect species in the tropical forests. To give you a feel for these numbers let us compare two countries of similar size with differing climates—tropical Guyana in South America (Figure 2.7) and temperate Britain. Table 2.1 compares various features of the two countries. Guyana is a country dominated by tropical forest, with about 80% of its surface area being covered by forest.

Table 2.1   Some comparisons of Britain and Guyana. The total number of insect species in Guyana is unknown.

	Britain	Guyana
climate	temperate	tropical
area	244 000 km^2	215 000 km^2
number of butterfly species*	59	>900
number of all insect species	about 23 000	?

* Not all the butterfly and other insect species will be associated with forest/woodland habitat.

Mainly because of their attractiveness and ease of collection, butterflies have been very thoroughly collected world-wide and are therefore one of the few insect groups for which we can reliably estimate the number of species in the tropics. However, even for this insect group in Guyana we are likely to be underestimating the number by several hundred species. Because many entomologists have been working in Britain for so long we can make a good guess at the total number of insect species (of all types) in Britain (Table 2.1). Now let us make a *crude* assumption and use the known difference in numbers of butterfly species in the two countries (Table 2.1) to predict the (unknown) number of all insect species in Guyana.

▷ Based on the difference in numbers of butterfly species between Guyana and Britain, estimate the total number of insect species in Guyana.

▶ There is at least a 900/59, i.e. approximately 15-fold, difference in numbers of butterfly species between the two countries. *If* this difference is the same for all insect species, there would be about $15 \times 23\,000$, i.e. 345\,000 insect species in Guyana.

This is typical of the type of educated guess which has to be made in the absence of reliable field data! Indeed, one of the main reasons why the estimation of the total number of species world-wide is highly contentious is that we know so little about species such as insects in the tropical forests.

Estimates of current world rates of species extinction are based on the facts that (1) there are a large number of species associated with tropical moist forests, and (2) deforestation and degradation of tropical forest habitats are occurring at a particular (and alarming) rate. We will now look more closely at these data in an attempt to arrive at an estimate of how rapidly species are being lost. Table 2.2 shows the areas

Table 2.2 Areas of tropical moist forest in different parts of the world in 1980, and average annual rates of deforestation, 1976–1980 (hectares, ha, $\times 10^3$). Only the countries with more than 10 million hectares of forest are shown. Many of the data are based on satellite images. (1 hectare $\approx$ 2.5 acres, or $10^4\,\mathrm{m}^2$.)

	Area of forest/ $\times 10^3$ ha	Annual deforestation rate/$\times 10^3$ ha year^{-1}
Africa		
Cameroon	17\,920	80
Congo	21\,340	–
Gabon	20\,500	27
Madagascar	10\,300	165
Zaire	105\,650	165
total	204\,622	1\,204
Asia and Pacific		
Burma	31\,193	89
India	16\,739	48
Indonesia	113\,575	550
Malaysia	20\,995	240
Papua New Guinea	33\,710	21
total	263\,647	1\,608
Latin America		
Bolivia	44\,010	65
Brazil	331\,750	1\,360
Colombia	46\,400	800
Ecuador	14\,230	300
Guyana	18\,475	2.5
Mexico	14\,760	160
Peru	68\,778	160
Surinam	14\,830	2.5
Venezuela	31\,870	125
total	613\,103	3\,301
global total	1\,081\,372	6\,113

of tropical moist forest and the average annual rates of deforestation. However, these rates include only land used for agricultural 'development' and not, for example, those areas where logging is prevalent, a practice which itself reduces the number of species.

Activity 2.1   *You should spend up to 15 minutes on this activity.*

(a) Using the global totals in Table 2.2, what percentage of the total area of forest was being lost on average each year during the late 1970s?

(b) Suppose you were asked to identify from Table 2.2 the five countries that had the highest rates of deforestation. What two arithmetical approaches (yielding different answers) could be adopted?

(c) Identify the 'top' five countries using both the methods of calculation identified in (b).

(d) What general conclusions do you feel emerge from the answers to (b) and (c)?

With estimates of the average loss of tropical forests per year, the total number of species in the world and the fraction of those species in the tropical forest, we can attempt to estimate the rate of species extinctions in tropical forests. For the purpose of this exercise we will use two estimates of the total number of species on Earth. The first is 1.8 million species, which is approximately the number which have been described and named. The second estimate of 10 million is the total number of described and unknown (guessed) species, although a few scientists have made much higher 'guestimates'.

Question 2.3   If it is *assumed* that numbers of species are reduced *in direct proportion* to the amount of habitat lost, then it is possible to estimate the loss of species *per day* in tropical forests during the late 1970s. Estimate this expected loss, based on the two estimates of 1.8 million and 10 million species world-wide and the value given earlier, for the proportion of world species found in tropical forests.

▷   What important assumptions were made in Question 2.3 in order to estimate the species extinction rates?

▶   That half of the world's species were found in tropical forests and that these species were lost *in direct proportion* to habitat loss. This last assumption is unlikely to be correct and we will return to it in Chapter 6.

The estimates of species loss in Question 2.3 may, however, be on the conservative side, due to logging etc.

This chapter began by pointing out that in the latter part of the 20th century, exceptional levels of species extinction are being witnessed. Implicit in this statement is the fact that humans are contributing to much of the loss. This statement can be verified only if we know the 'background' rates of extinction, i.e. those prior to the influence of humans. It is important to remember that species extinction is a natural process which can occur in the absence of humans. The *average* background levels estimated, from fossils, over the past 600 million years are of about *one* species extinction *per year*, i.e. thousands of times less than those estimated above. We should, however, be as cautious about this estimate as we are of present day extinction rates, perhaps even more so. It is likely to be too low, as we have little information on the losses of non-fossilizable species. Despite that lack of information it is still difficult to imagine rates of loss anywhere near those happening now.

2.2.2 Temperate woodland

The present levels of tropical deforestation are quite rightly raising concerns about the rate of species extinction. Your own reactions to tropical deforestation may be tempered or exacerbated as you learn more about the behaviour of some of our ancestors in Britain, a subject to which we now turn. In 1830, the historian Thomas Carlyle wrote:

Whoever was up-rooting a thistle, or bramble, or draining a bog, or building himself a house, that man was writing the history of England.

(Peter Brandon, 1974, *The Sussex Landscape*)

In these terms, the history of England was almost entirely written by the 14th century, when most of the woodland which had covered lowland England following the end of the last glaciation (*c.* 8 000 BC) had been removed. The removal of the temperate forest in England began in earnest with the arrival of Neolithic farmers (*c.* 3 000 BC), although there is evidence that earlier Mesolithic peoples (*c.* 8 000–4 000 BC), who were primarily hunters, cleared woodland by means of fire to increase the open areas in which they could hunt their prey.

In lowland England, the process of deforestation continued after the Romano-British period, with less accessible and less easily worked areas of woodland being cleared. The height of the woodland clearance appears to have been during the 13th and 14th centuries. By 1348, according to Peter Brandon, 'little more virgin woodland remained to fall to the foresters axe'. It is this impression of a largely denuded landscape with which we are left today. Along with the woodland has gone the wolf, wild boar, bear and beaver. Only the occasional pockets of 'ancient' woodland remain, whilst the few large tracts of woodland which avoided clearance did so due to their protection as, for example, former hunting parks. Brandon, in his assessment of the history of the Sussex landscape, wrote:

It seems therefore that almost all of the open country in Sussex has been created by man in the process of progressive deforestation which in England led to the virtual destruction of deciduous woodland.

The effect of deforestation depended on the soil type underlying the cleared vegetation. In lowland southern England, we can consider two rock types, chalk and sand, which give rise to very different soil types. The distribution of these rock types in the county of Sussex is shown in Figure 2.8. With the loss of the woodland in southern England, two new habitats began to replace the former extensive woodland cover. Heaths developed on the sandy soils, whilst the chalk soils became covered with areas of grassland. Figure 2.9 shows the distribution of two plant species, the cross-leaved heath (*Erica tetralix*) and the horseshoe vetch (*Hippocrepis comosa*), that are limited to particular types of soil in Sussex.

▷ Compare Figures 2.8 and 2.9, and decide to which soil-determined habitats the two plant species are limited.

▶ The horseshoe vetch is limited to soils overlying chalk and the cross-leaved heath is limited to sandy (acidic) soils.

Today these two habitats—heathlands and chalk grasslands—are themselves rare and declining, once again endangered by human activities. For example, much of the chalk grassland has been ploughed up and 'improved' for agriculture with artificial fertilizers during the past 50 years. This in turn jeopardizes the survival of plant and animal species associated with chalk grassland. These species include the early gentian, *Gentianella anglica*, one of the few species restricted to Britain and not also found in mainland Europe.

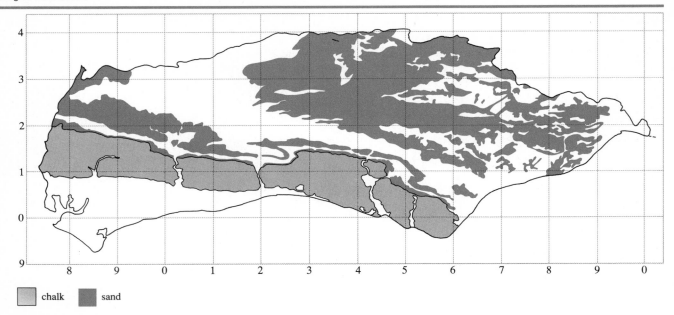

chalk   sand

Figure 2.8 Distribution of chalk and sand in Sussex. The rock type, in influencing soil pH and composition, helps to determine the type of vegetation growing in that area.

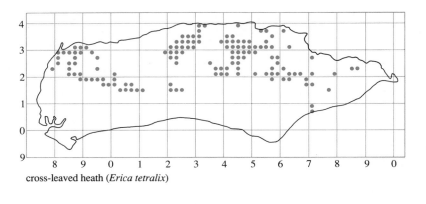

cross-leaved heath (*Erica tetralix*)

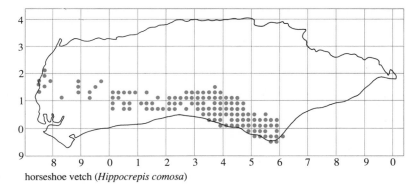

horseshoe vetch (*Hippocrepis comosa*)

Figure 2.9 The distribution of the cross-leaved heath (*Erica tetralix*), and the horseshoe vetch (*Hippocrepis comosa*) in Sussex.

▷   What clue is there in the early gentian's scientific name which identifies its geographic range?

▶   The species name *anglica* indicates that it is restricted to England, although this is not always reliable—*Gentianella germanica* also occurs in England!

The large-scale removal of temperate woodland in western Europe and elsewhere offers a vision of the end-point of the deforestation in tropical countries. Unfortunately, the reality in many tropical countries is likely to be far worse because levels of soil erosion and nutrient loss (particularly in upland areas) are generally much higher than when temperate woodland is cleared.

2.3 Responding to the losses

In this section we are concerned with a major question raised in Chapter 1: what type of scientific response is appropriate to the problem of species extinction and habitat loss? First, it is necessary to monitor precisely the rates of loss to clarify the extent of the problem. Second, if the outcome of the monitoring points to a problem, conservationists need to consider how the rate of species and habitat loss may be reduced. The aim of this section is to describe briefly some methods by which losses (and sometimes gains!) are monitored, and point to the means by which such losses may be reduced or even reversed. In our attempt to define and describe conservation, we will look at such issues here in a preliminary way, and many of the points raised will be looked at again in Chapters 4 and 5.

2.3.1 Monitoring species and habitats

Monitoring involves the recording of changes in the abundance of species or habitats. The scale and amount of technology involved varies widely, as implied by Plates 2.1 and 2.2 and Figure 2.10, which show three examples of monitoring techniques. Plate 2.1 shows images from a Landsat satellite of vegetation around Brighton in East Sussex, and Malham in North Yorkshire. The Landsat programme began in 1972 with the launch of the first satellite, Landsat 1, and its successors have generated a huge amount of information about the geology and vegetation of the Earth and the effects of humans upon it. This information can be interpreted in a variety of ways and in a range of applications; for example, many of the data in Table 2.2 were compiled from Landsat images.

In Plate 2.2 we see an example of monitoring which is decidedly 'low-tech' and from a closer vantage point than that of Landsat! This person, on his hands and knees, is recording the abundance of plant species by counting the number of plants in a fixed area. Despite the simplicity of this method it is the basis for much of the evaluation of species and habitats, as will become clear in Chapter 4. The types of monitoring shown in Plates 2.1 and 2.2 not only represent the two ends of the technology spectrum but also two extremes of spatial scale. In Plate 2.1 monitoring is at a resolution of tens of metres, whilst in Plate 2.2 the monitoring is at a scale of millimetres.

Another dimension—that of time—is added to the monitoring process in Figure 2.10. As mentioned in Section 2.2.1, current species and habitat losses need to be weighed against past losses. This is possible only if we have a detailed knowledge of the past changes, such as details of the fossil record. Whilst the fossil record is measured over millions of years, the records shown in Figure 2.10 refer to thousands of years. In this technique, cores through soil or lake sediments are taken and the abundance and species identity of pollen in the sediments recorded. The strata from which pollen are taken are then dated to provide a picture of how the vegetation has changed over time. For example, *Betula* species appear to be more abundant at the start and end of the interglacial, suggesting that they prefer relatively cooler climates. The species composition and extent of the primeval forest which covered most of western Europe following the last glaciation is known through evidence of pollen records.

Combinations of techniques such as those depicted in Plates 2.1 and 2.2, and Figure 2.10, and the fossil record therefore allow us to monitor changes in a square metre of

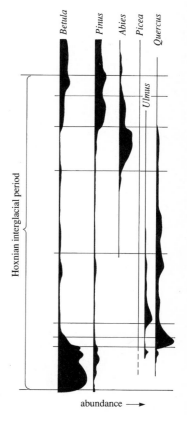

Figure 2.10 An example of species and habitat monitoring. Evidence of interglacial vegetation change from pollen preserved in a 17-metre core from lake sediments in Marks Tey in Essex. The period covered is about 17 000 years (the Hoxnian interglacial, which occurred about 400 000 years ago). The names refer to genera of plants: *Betula* (birch), *Pinus* (pine), *Abies* (fir), *Picea* (spruce), *Ulmus* (elm) and *Quercus* (oak). For further explanation see the text.

turf or the whole planet over a few days, years or millions of years (but obviously at different levels of resolution).

What happens when the monitoring exercises indicate that species or habitat losses are too high? Perhaps a species appears to be rapidly disappearing from a number of locations, or satellite images over several years have recorded a continuing decline of a particular habitat. Often, the greatest hurdle is not one with which science can assist. Economic or land-use conflicts stand in the way of many effective responses to conservation problems. If we assume that these problems have been overcome, then there are two clear options available: protection and/or management.

2.3.2 Protection and management

Protection, at its crudest, simply involves demarcating an area and preventing the factors which are causing the species or habitat loss (e.g. hunting, deforestation, pollution) from continuing. This option is a first step in the process of halting or reversing species or habitat loss, but is frequently not used in isolation. Environmental law is not covered in this book but science is required to help in the drafting of sensible environmental legislation, for example, specifying the number and size of protected areas. Coupled with this protection is management of the habitat or species.

It often appears contradictory that in order to prevent the demise of one species or habitat we have to manage it in a way which may reduce the abundance of other species! In Britain, the preservation of rare plants in chalk grassland (itself a habitat created by humans—see Section 2.2.2) requires cutting or grazing the grassland to prevent the encroachment of trees into the area. In other words, this involves mimicking the 'management' of the area (i.e. maintaining the deforestation) by our predecessors, who created the habitat in the first place, is necessary. The details of some present-day management procedures will become clear in Chapter 5, though the underlying principles for grassland are straightforward enough.

▷ Can you recall from the Australian example what would happen to many grasslands, left to their own devices?

▶ They would become woodland (Section 2.1.2).

This process of vegetation change is referred to as **succession** and is covered in detail in Chapter 5. Unless the area is managed—unless the inexorable process of tree invasion is slowed down—we will be left with little grassland and lots of scrub and woodland. Surely, you will say, this is a good thing. We need more trees, as in other places they are being lost at an alarming rate; furthermore, this is what the original landscape was like before the interference of humans. The answer to this conundrum (although the 'answer' really dodges the issue) is that humans have to make choices—we are able to both destroy and create habitats. We can maintain the grassland through management such as sheep grazing, and promote the growth of otherwise rare grassland plants. Conversely, we can leave grassland to return to scrub and woodland—we can even accelerate that process by adding tree seeds and excluding natural grazers such as rabbits. From a purely scientific point of view the choice is ours. These choices may need to be made in the light of the long-term history of the site and the conflicts with other land uses, but they are our choices and should be made in an informed and objective way. Hopefully, by the time you reach the end of this book you will be able to appreciate more clearly the criteria upon which such choices are made.

2.4 Conclusion: defining biological conservation

This chapter has discussed the problems facing conservation scientists and their responses to these problems.

▷ Can you suggest a single-sentence definition for biological conservation?

▶ One possibility is 'the study of the change in the biological composition of the world, and the development and application of methods for altering that change'.

Normally change is going to mean loss, so biological conservation will be concerned with reducing or reversing that decline. Inherent in this argument is that reducing or reversing that decline is a good thing, a subject to which we return in Chapter 3.

Summary of Chapter 2

1   The primary problems of biological conservation are species extinction and habitat loss.

2   Responses by conservationists to these problems are divided into monitoring (which objectively clarifies the extent of the problem), management and protection.

3   Species extinction and habitat loss are linked phenomena—the latter is often a cause of the former, along with other factors such as hunting.

4   Whilst it is clear that species extinctions and habitat losses are occurring, it is difficult to determine the rate of loss, particularly of species, because of our lack of knowledge of species-rich habitats such as the tropical moist forests.

5   Monitoring of the change in species numbers and habitat size is undertaken at different spatial scales, using a variety of technologies, from pollen counts in sediment cores to satellite images. The changes which can be identified by these methods occur over a wide range of timescales.

6   When potential or actual species or habitat losses are identified, the next step is usually to implement management and/or protection policies. Management of terrestrial habitats is often achieved by controlling the natural succession from grassland to woodland.

Question 2.4 Fill in the gaps in the following paragraph:

Balaenoptera musculus (blue whale) and *Balaenoptera physalus* (fin whale) are examples of two species. in the same genus. They share a common habitat in the oceans of the world. The small group of blue whale individuals living in the North Atlantic Ocean can be considered to be a single population

Question 2.5 State, in general terms, two problems associated with attempting to *quantify* the effect of loss of habitat (e.g. tropical moist forest) on species numbers.

Question 2.6 Give one simple way in which a named form of management can alter ecological succession.

3 Why conserve?

In Chapters 1 and 2 it was generally assumed that species extinction and habitat loss are undesirable and therefore that conservation of endangered species and habitats is to be encouraged. In this chapter, several reasons for conserving species and habitats will be considered. Some of these reasons have little or no scientific content, which implies we can cover them only in passing, whilst those highlighted in Sections 3.2 and 3.3 have a strong scientific basis.

3.1 Aesthetics

For many people, the reason to conserve the world's species and habitats is that they constitute beautiful objects or landscapes within and amongst which it is possible to escape the dreariness of day-to-day urban life. This was certainly the view of many Victorian naturalists who, whilst not being explicitly conservationists, were motivated by a love of natural objects—often, as they saw it, revealing the artistry and beauty of their Creator. Philip Gosse, an eminent Victorian naturalist, wrote in his book *The Romance of Natural History* (1860):

> *There are more ways than one of studying natural history. There is Dr Dryas-dust's way—which consists of mere accuracy of definition and differentiation; statistics as harsh and dry as the skin and bones in the museum where it is studied. There is the field observer's way: the careful and conscientious accumulation and record of facts bearing on the life-history of the creatures; statistics as fresh and bright as the forest or meadow from which they are gathered in the dewy morning. And there is the poet's way, who looks at nature through a glass peculiarly his own; the aesthetic aspect, which deals, not with statistics, but with the emotions of the human mind—surprise, wonder, terror, revulsion, admiration, love, desire, and so forth—which are made energetic by the contemplation of the creatures around him.*

Orchids provide an example of plants that have great aesthetic appeal. In Britain there are about 50 species of orchid—some examples are shown in Plate 3.1. Orchid species are often described as the most beautiful and unusual plants and have generated great interest amongst naturalists. The herbalist John Gerard described, in 1597, the various kinds of 'Fox-stones' (orchids):

> *There be divers kindes of Fox-stones, differing very much in shape of their leaves, as also in floures: some have floures, wherein is to be seen the shape of sundry sorts of living creatures*; some the shape and proportion of flies, in other gnats, some humble bees, others like unto honey Bees; some like Butter-flies, and others like Waspes that be dead; some yellow of colour, others white; some purple mixed with red, others of a brown overworne colour ... There is no great use of these in*

---

* One feature of orchids is their unusual methods of pollination. A bizarre and often quoted mechanism, which relates to Gerard's description, is that of pseudo-copulation. In this pollination system the flower is assumed to resemble a small insect such as a bee. These pollinating animals are then attracted to this flower by its colour, shape and smell in the belief that they have located a mate. They attempt to mate with the flower and in so doing collect its pollen. This is a good story; unfortunately, the evidence for pseudo-copulation is rather scanty.

physicke, but they are chiefly regarded for the pleasant and beautifull floures wherewith Nature hath seemed to play and disport her selfe.

(M. Woodward, 1985, *Gerard's Herbal*)

These aesthetic properties of the orchid species have led to their being higher profile candidates for conservation than say, an ugly spider (though some people find spiders beautiful, and a few rare species, such as the raft spider—the largest British species— are the subjects of intense conservation activity). Of course, the fact that orchids are aesthetically pleasing has led to them being over-collected and this has undoubtedly contributed to the decline of many species. The problem still occurs through legal and illegal international trade into Britain, particularly in tropical species. Victorian naturalists collected orchids and other visually striking species avidly, which is one reason why tropical butterflies (another group of aesthetically pleasing organisms) are so well known (Section 2.2.1). Arguably our most famous orchid, the lady's slipper orchid or *Cypripedium calceolus* L. (Plate 3.1a), was sufficiently abundant in Britain 100 years ago to have been collected in large numbers. Now there is only a single plant remaining in Britain, although it is still found in a number of large colonies in mainland Europe.

3.2 Knowledge

Some of our most important discoveries about the natural world (including ourselves) have come about precisely because we have had large areas of natural world to examine and compare. Whilst we may be able to exist in a species-poor world, it will not be a place within which the 19th century founders of modern evolutionary theory (Charles Darwin and Alfred Russel Wallace) would have flourished. The theory of evolution depends on two key sets of observations of the natural world. First, that there is variation between organisms (some of which is heritable). Second, given that variation, certain individuals do better in terms of survival and reproduction than others when exposed to a common natural threat, such as a predator. **Natural selection** is the name given to the process determining this differential survival in the face of a common threat. Consider, for example, two plant individuals of the same species; the one which has a slightly better chemical defence against herbivores may survive to produce more offspring than the plant with the less effective defence. Natural selection can therefore be said to 'favour' plants with the better chemical defence. As you can appreciate, the details of these processes are much more complicated than this but the key point in the present context is that *variation* is a vital component of evolution; indeed, natural selection can work only in the presence of variation.

One of the most conspicuous examples of variation within and between animal species comes from the colour and patterns of colour in butterflies. An important discovery was that some brightly coloured butterflies are often unpalatable or toxic, and that their bold colours act as advertisements of this fact.

▷ To whom are these brightly coloured butterflies advertising?

▶ To potential predators. In effect, they are saying 'don't eat me, I contain toxin'.

These toxins often come from the food plants upon which the larvae of the butterflies have fed. Henry Bates, working in the 1860s in South American tropical forests where butterfly species richness reaches its greatest heights, made an important discovery. Not all of the species with apparent warning colouration were actually toxic!

▷ What is the benefit to the brightly coloured butterflies of *not* containing toxins?

▶ They can have the advantage of protection from predators without having to expend energy on either manufacturing the toxin or using the toxins of their host plants.

In effect, these butterfly species are cheating, mimicking the colours of their unpalatable counterparts. As Bates and others continued their work they discovered this was not the end of the story. It became clear that there were 'mimicry complexes' containing up to ten (occasionally more) species in the same area (Plate 3.2), from a number of different butterfly families, involved in *two* types of mimicry. There were those mimics that pretended to be unpalatable but were not (Batesian mimics), and there were those that *were* unpalatable and used the same advertising colours as others that were also unpalatable (Müllerian mimics).

▷ What is the benefit to individuals of Müllerian mimicry?

▶ By wearing a 'common badge' they would reinforce the fact that they were unpalatable to shared predators.

Natural selection, along with other mechanisms, has ensured, over many generations of these insects, that the mimics and the mimicked have become very similar in colour. Our knowledge of the operation of natural selection in this instance (and therefore of further evidence of the mechanisms of evolution) could not have come about in the species-poor habitats which occur after large-scale deforestation.

This is but one of many examples which could have been used to show the importance of species-rich habitats in revealing the way natural selection has operated. In Chapter 6 we return to the requirement of maintaining species-rich habitats, for rather different reasons than those revealed here. Finally, explicit in this section has been the idea that as we lose individuals and species and therefore variation we lose knowledge. Not only that but we lose the variation upon which *future* natural selection may operate—a point made very forcefully by Norman Myers in *The Guardian* (24 April 1992).

> *True, evolution will eventually come up with replacement species. But for evolution to generate an array of species that will match today's in numbers and diversity will require a recovery period extending for at least 200 000 human generations into the future—or 20 times more generations than have existed since humankind itself emerged as a species. More specifically, we are almost certainly determining there shall be no new forms of the great cats and apes, rhinos and pandas and many other species.*

3.3 Plant and animal resources

The habitats of the world may be thought of as stores of a range of **biological resources** useful to humans. These resources come from various parts of a wide selection of both plant and animal species. Thus, plants from forests and grasslands provide food, medicines and building materials from their roots, leaves, stems and flowers whilst animals may provide meat, clothing and medicinal products. Tables 3.1 and 3.2 give examples of some of the resources available and their origins.

Table 3.1 Examples of animal resources.

Examples of use	Resource (part of animal)	Name of species	Continents of origin
shoes	skin	two caiman species (types of crocodile)	South America
ornaments	ivory products, from tusks	African elephant	Africa (see Section 3.3.2)
'medicinal' purposes	horn/variety of organs	five rhinoceros species	two in Africa, three in south-east Asia
coats	skin/fur	ocelot and other cat species	South America

Table 3.2 Examples of plant resources.

Examples of use	Resource (part of plant)	Name of species	Countries of origin (though often cultivated elsewhere)
food (starch)	seed (grain)	rice (*Oryza sativa*)	India/China
food (starch)	root tuber	sweet potato (*Ipomoea batatus*)	South America (probably)
food (protein/oil)	seed (48% protein, 19% oil)	soya (*Glycine max*)	south-east Asia
food (protein/oil)	seed (18% protein, 60% oil)	Brazil or Para nut (*Bertholletia excelsa*)	Brazil! Also found in Bolivia, Peru, Ecuador, Colombia and Venezuela
rubber	latex	various species such as Para rubber (*Hevea brasiliensis*)	Brazil
insulating and water-repellant material	hairs from inside seed pod	kapok or silk-cotton (*Ceiba pentandra*)	South and Central America

Virtually all habitats in the world have been exploited in some way as various human groups have sought uses for biological resources. The following quotation from John Terborgh's book *Five New World Primates. A Study in Comparative Ecology* (1983), relating to his work in the tropical rainforest of South America, is a powerful example of the extent of biological resource use:

> *This study would never have taken place were it not for our 'discovery' of Cocha Cashu in 1973. At that time I had been travelling in Peru and other South American countries for ten years, but had never before seen a place in the lowlands that was utterly pristine. While this may seem surprising in view of the vast expanse of primary lowland forest that remains in Amazonia to this day, the fact is that nearly all of it has been exploited in one way or another, for game, furs, natural rubber, Brazil nuts, prime timber etc. Animal populations are especially vulnerable to the slightest encroachment, and appear to melt away before seemingly insignificant human populations. This is because of the devastating effectiveness of modern firearms. A skilled hunter equipped with a standard one-shot 16-gauge shotgun can single-handedly eliminate large birds and mammals within a radius of several hours walk from his dwelling. So, even if the forest looks lush and intact from the air, the appearance is deceptive, much of it is a hollow shell so far as animals are concerned.*

Having only seen places which were exposed to hunting, I was not fully aware of this. It was the contrast of Cocha Cashu that put all my previous experience in perspective. Animals are actually plentiful, especially primates. Never before had I seen so many monkeys of so many species, much less monkeys that did not flee at the first hint of a human being.

In Chapter 2 it was suggested that, alongside habitat loss, hunting is a major contributor to species extinction. Many valued biological resources can be obtained only by killing individuals, which in turn can contribute to the demise of the species. There are several reasons why large-bodied animal and plant species are especially vulnerable. First, compared with smaller species, they have a higher yield of product relative to the effort of hunting. They will also be more conspicuous and therefore more easily hunted and killed (given suitable tools such as rifles or chainsaws). In addition, larger bodied species generally have lower rates of population increase than smaller bodied species. To illustrate the vulnerability of large species, the next two sections describe some examples of exploitation that are at the forefront of public concern.

3.3.1 The decline of the blue whale

The largest bodied animal, the blue whale (*Balaenoptera musculus*), weighs up to 178 tonnes and can reach 30 m in length. Its numbers declined dramatically from 1930 to 1959; ironically the evidence for the decline in numbers came from information on reduced catches (Figure 3.1).

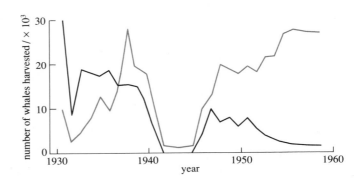

Figure 3.1 The number of blue whales (black line) and fin whales (green line), both *Balaenoptera* sp., caught (harvested) in the period 1930–1959.

Question 3.1 What are the three most striking features of the changes in the harvested numbers of blue and fin whales illustrated in Figure 3.1?

Question 3.2 What assumption needs to be made if the number of blue whales caught are taken to be indicative of the total number of blue whales in the oceans?

Today the blue whale is highly endangered, with an estimated total number of only 6000–7000; smaller individuals are now much more common in the population than previously. A major problem that contributed to the decline of the blue whale was its very low population growth rate.

▷   What are the causes of a low population growth rate?

▶   Population growth rates are determined by the rate at which offspring are born and the chances of survival of individuals. The blue whale has high rates of survival in the absence of hunting but very slow rates of offspring production (the gestation period is about 1 year, females are not sexually mature until about 5 years, and only one calf is born at a time).

These features of slow production of offspring are shared by all large-bodied mammals, including the African elephant. In the absence of hunting this does not pose a problem, but when even moderate numbers are killed it means that the populations are very slow, or unable, to recover.

3.3.2 The decline of the African elephant

In the latter half of the 20th century the largest bodied terrestrial animal, the African elephant (*Loxodonta africana*), has also shown a rapid decrease in numbers. We will spend some time discussing the fate of the African elephant, as it clearly demonstrates the effect of exploitation of a resource, ivory (Table 3.1), on abundance of the species providing the resource.

Animals are killed in order to remove the tusks which are used to make ivory products. Tusk weight is highest amongst large males (each tusk weighs an average of 9.3 kg). Large males may weigh up to 6 000 kg or 6 tonnes (light compared with the largest blue whale!).

As large males have been culled preferentially, so the population structure, defined as the proportion of individuals of a given age, size and sex, has changed, resulting in populations dominated by females and younger animals. Young and female animals have in turn been culled for ivory, so the average tusk weight has declined further. These effects have been particularly apparent during the 1980s. Data on the export of ivory in the 1980s are given in Table 3.3.

▷ If the average tusk weight varies from 9.3 kg (large males) to 4.7 kg (females and small males), how many dead elephants are represented by one tonne of ivory?

▶ The equivalent average number of elephants is found by dividing one tonne (1 000 kg) by 18.6 kg (two tusks per elephant) or 9.4 kg. One tonne of ivory therefore represents between 54 and 106 dead elephants.

Table 3.3   The top five ivory exporting countries, 1979–1987. These data show the mass of ivory exported (kg) and the equivalent number of dead elephants, based on average tusk weights of 9.3 and 4.7 kg. It is likely that these export values are underestimates, although some attempt has been made to include illegal hunting in the data. Note that exporting countries do not necessarily contain large elephant populations.

Country	Total ivory exported/kg	9.3 ($\times 2$) kg elephant equivalents	4.7 ($\times 2$) kg elephant equivalents
Sudan	1 451 599	78 043	154 425
Central African Republic	1 136 257	61 089	120 878
Burundi	1 084 014	58 280	115 321
Congo	931 925	50 103	99 141
Zaire	672 088	36 134	71 499
total, including other African countries	7 482 870	402 305	796 050

We can now compare the losses in Table 3.3 due to legal and illegal hunting with the change in the numbers of live animals recorded by various techniques (described in Extract 3.1 and Chapter 4) over the period 1981–1989 (Table 3.4). Table 3.4 therefore covers the same amount of time as Table 3.3 but starts 2 years later. Direct comparison between Tables 3.3 and 3.4 on a region by region basis is difficult, so we will concentrate on the decline in the total population of African elephants (Table 3.4) and on the total export of ivory from Africa (Table 3.3).

Table 3.4 Change in size of African elephant population, 1981–1989. The 1981 numbers are likely to be underestimates, whilst the 1989 numbers are more accurate, so this change represents a minimum decline. East Africa, where the largest decline was seen, includes Tanzania and Sudan (both with >70% loss during the 1980s).

Region	Estimated population size		% change between 1981 and 1989
	1981	1989	
Central Africa	436 200	277 000	−36.5
East Africa	429 500	110 000	−74.4
South Africa	309 000	204 000	−34.0
West Africa	17 600	15 700	−10.8
total	1 192 300	606 700	−49.1

Question 3.3 By considering the *total* numbers of elephants in Table 3.4 in 1981–1989, and the *total* amount of ivory exported and equivalent number of dead elephants in Table 3.3, what single conclusion can you deduce about the effects of hunting for ivory on the size of the elephant population during the 1980s?

▷ Why would you not expect to see an exact match between the loss in elephant numbers during the 1980s and the numbers apparently lost due to hunting for ivory?

▶ There is a time-lag of 2 years between numbers lost due to ivory hunting (Table 3.3) and estimates of population size (Table 3.4). There are also inaccuracies both in extrapolating from ivory weight to number of individuals, and in the estimates of the size of the elephant populations (see Chapter 4). Finally, we cannot be certain about the exact amount of ivory exported.

Despite these inaccuracies, the data reveal unequivocally that hunting for ivory in the 1980s was a primary factor causing the dramatic decline in African elephant numbers.

Activity 3.1   *You should spend up to 1 hour on this activity.*

Extract 3.1 is the major part of an article that explores some of the issues associated with the conservation of the African elephant. In particular, it focuses on recent attempts to remove the African elephant from the list of internationally-agreed 'fully protected' species (agreed in 1989, and prohibiting legal trading in ivory) to a lower category of protection, thereby enabling commercial ivory trading to recommence.

First, read the entire extract, trying to apply what you know already about extracting the essential information from a text such as this. Remember that a useful 'orientation' tactic is to read the first one or two sentences of each paragraph carefully to find a key word or phrase. In addition, make notes, or annotate the article, or use underlining and/or a highlighting pen—any device that aids concentration and helps you to identify and remember the sequence of ideas and facts being put forward.

Now assess your grasp of the content of Extract 3.1 by answering (a) and (b).

(a) Summarize the arguments (i) *for* and (ii) *against* the proposal for a relaxation of the 1989 ban on ivory trading. In each case, present your answer in the form of a list of notes divided under the three headings: scientific, economic, and others.

(b) Now use a selection of this information to present a concise and well-argued point of view. Do this by writing a letter to a newspaper, of no more than 250 words, *opposing* any relaxation of the ban on ivory trading. Concentrate in your letter on the underlying *scientific* justification for your point of view.

[handwritten margin note:] Much of the reduction in numbers can be accounted for by culling for ivory.

Extract 3.1   From *New Scientist*, 29 February 1992, pp. 29–33.

Conservation and the ivory tower

Is commerce the enemy of conservation? Next week representatives from around the world meet to reconcile the interests of endangered species and those who would exploit them.

David Concar and Mary Cole

Would-be traders in ivory and illicit furs will be holding their breath next week as delegates gather in Kyoto, Japan, for the biennial Convention on International Trade in Endangered Species. Among those vying for a place on the CITES ark this year will be creatures as diverse as the arctic bear, whose gall bladders are in demand by practitioners of traditional Asian medicine, and the bog turtle, which is under pressure from the pet trade and the spread of golf courses through its north American habitats. Even the humble herring and the mahogany tree will be discussed as part of a bold attempt to extend the treaty's authority beyond rare wildlife. Yet, for all this, it will be the African elephant which attracts most publicity and the bulk of delegates' time, just as it did when CITES last met. The long-running dispute over how best to conserve the largest land mammal in the world is about to erupt all over again.

At issue is the trade ban on ivory imposed by CITES in 1989 after a decade of heavy poaching. This ban is now up for review, and Zimbabwe and five other southern African countries—Botswana, Namibia, Malawi, South Africa and Zambia—will be lobbying hard in Kyoto for a partial relaxation. They want to downgrade their own elephant populations from the convention's Appendix 1, its list of the wholly sacrosanct, to Appendix 2, which permits regulated trade in some animal products. What they have in mind is a strictly controlled trade in ivory, involving just one exporter—a cartel of ivory producing nations—and one major importer, Japan.

Conservationists in eastern and central Africa, along with many wildlife pressure groups, are up in arms over the proposal. Such a move, they fear, could revive the poaching epidemic which the 1989 ban curbed so successfully. For them, the pressing issue is what steps in addition to the ban should be taken to prevent *Loxodonta africana* going the same way as its evolutionary cousins, the mammoths and mastodonts.

Heightening the conflict over ivory will be a range of other provocative proposals from the southern African cartel. All but South Africa want to relax a long-standing ban on commercial trade in leopard skins, for instance, while Namibia and Zimbabwe are trying to downlist the cheetah. Four of the countries want to reopen trade in various bodily parts of the endangered Cape pangolin, an anteater whose scales are used in traditional Chinese medicine and whose flesh is considered a delicacy in many parts of Africa. The rhinoceros is likely to stir debate, too. Zimbabwe and South Africa are pressing for a relaxation of the current trade ban on rhino horn, arguing that their own rhinoceros populations are now secure enough to be downlisted to Appendix 2. Both countries have built up large stockpiles of rhino horn as a result of dehorning programmes aimed at deterring poachers. Now they would like to sell them off.

Behind all these proposals is a single, simple philosophy: African wildlife, if it is to survive in the long run, must pay its way. And for the proponents of this philosophy the elephant has taken on symbolic value in the struggle to put it into practice. Thus, conservationists in Zimbabwe talk of 'farming' their elephant herds as a 'sustainable resource', harvesting not only tusks but hides and meat, too. The revenue so generated, they argue—which could run into several million dollars per year—could be ploughed back into conservation. By contrast, countries such as Kenya see tourism, rather than trade, as the key to saving Africa's large mammals.

This clash of ideas is born of a long-standing paradox. While successive waves of poaching in the 1970s and 1980s forced countless elephant populations in central and eastern Africa to the brink of extinction, elephants in Zimbabwe and South Africa continued to multiply inside well-protected national parks. So much so, in fact, that they soon became a threat to the very habitat that sustains them. In the Hwange National Park, home to most of Zimbabwe's elephants since the late 1960s, annual culls designed to reduce pressure on vegetation have since become the norm.

When CITES last grappled with the paradox, in 1989, the need to halt poaching prevailed. But since then pressure has grown for trade to be resumed. One reason, say western pressure groups such as Greenpeace and the Environmental Investigation Agency (EIA), is that Zimbabwe is culling more elephants than ever before and is thus building up an ever larger stockpile of ivory it cannot sell. Activists and the public alike have long challenged Zimbabwe's policy of culling elephants, and in the run-up to this year's CITES meeting their opposition has deepened. Anger erupted in January when it emerged that Zimbabwe plans to shoot as many as 5 000 elephants a year for the next 14 years.

The EIA immediately branded these culls as the 'largest state-sanctioned kill of elephants in history'. But wildlife scientists in Zimbabwe insist they are only doing what is necessary to prevent wholesale destruction of vegetation. The country's elephant population has doubled since the mid-1980s, they claim, and now stands at 68 000 animals, about 25 000 more than its scrublands can support. The conservation activists say Zimbabwe's scientists have got their sums wrong. The figure of 68 000, they charge, includes thousands of immigrant elephants from Botswana and Mozambique, which have moved into Zimbabwe to take advantage of watering holes and the space created by previous culls. Zimbabwe's scientists reject this notion, arguing that their figures are based on simultaneous counts of elephants on both sides of the border. They also insist that their aerial counting methods are no different from those used by wildlife scientists in the USA, Australia and Kenya (see Box 1), and that a panel of experts sent by CITES is satisfied with their data.

Zimbabwe's sympathisers say the country has simply become a victim of its own success in protecting elephants. Yet this defence is unlikely to quell accusations in Kyoto that its

1: Fishing for jumbo numbers

THE usual way to take a census of elephants from the air is to count all the animals that lie along a set of "transects", imaginary lines that crisscross the survey area. The first step is to select a survey area that will yield a precise estimate of the total population, preferably one with a relatively high density of elephants. Elephants are seldom evenly distributed, and either a preliminary flight over the area or a rough ground survey are usually necessary to stratify different areas according to their elephant densities.

"With limited time and money there is little point in intensively sampling known low-density areas," says Deborah Gibson, a consultant ecologist who previously worked in Zimbabwe's Department of National Parks.

Next, a baseline is drawn on a map, parallel to a major feature such as a river. Counting animals along the line of the river itself may produce biased results as they tend to gather at river banks at certain times of the day. The first transect is drawn perpendicular to the baseline, through a randomly placed point. The other transects are then placed parallel to the first transect, and at equal distances. The higher the estimated density of elephants in the area, the more transects are needed.

The observers fly along the transect lines, counting animals in strips 100 to 200 metres wide. In Botswana, these strips are marked out by fishing rods clamped to the plane's struts, two observers counting the game between the struts. Pilots have recently started using satellite naivigation equipment to help them keep on course.

Range of the African elephant, according to data compiled by the EC African Elephant Survey and Conservation Programme

Kenya

Zimbabwe

Hwange National Park

In Zimbabwe, counts are done in the dry season, from late August through to October, when most trees are leafless and animals more visible. "It is a very boring, tedious and tiring job and it is possible to miss game," says one observer. Moreover, resources are limited. It takes seven days to sample elephants in just 7 per cent of the 15 000 square kilometres of the Hwange National Park.

Where it is too hilly for transect counts from winged aircraft, block counts from a helicopter are done instead. Once again the whole area is first stratified according to elephant densities. Each stratum is then divided into small blocks, and a number of these are randomly selected. Observers fly over these blocks many times, counting the elephants within them.

When aerial counts began in Zimbabwe in 1967, observers would simply try to count every elephant they could see. As a result, the counts yielded estimates that were about one-third of the true population. The observers were searching so much ground that they were missing many animals. Today's methods, introduced in 1979, give more accurate estimates.

Every year conservationists in Zimbabwe still do ground surveys by going to water holes and counting the elephants that visit. National parks scientists argue that such counts are a waste of time because there is no guarantee that every animal will visit the waterholes, while some animals may be counted twice. Aerial photographs are impractical for counting elephants and video cameras do not have a fine enough resolution.

Counting forest-dwelling elephants is a greater challenge still as it cannot be done from the air. The most effective method requires certain detective skills. As part of wider research into elephant behaviour in the rainforests of Gabon, Richard Barnes, a zoologist at the University of Cambridge, and his colleagues have perfected the art of "counting by dung". Their approach is to number all the elephant dunghills in a selected area of forest, aging each one according to its state of decay. By combining this information with a knowledge of how often the local elephants defecate, the researchers can then estimate how many elephants live in the area. The diametres of the dunghills even give clues as to the elephants' sizes, and hence ages.

wildlife experts have failed to question their figures because they strengthen Zimbabwe's case in the ivory debate. Nor is the scepticism confined to pressure groups. Iain Douglas-Hamilton, who has spent a lifetime surveying and studying elephants in eastern Africa, doubts that the animals can reproduce fast enough to generate the kind of population increase Zimbabwe claims has taken place in its Hwange National Park in recent years.

But whatever their doubts about Zimbabwe's numbers, most elephant specialists view culling and the ivory trade as two separate issues. 'Culling is a purely internal affair, but the effects of the ivory trade go well beyond national borders,' says Stephen Cobb, of the African Elephant Conservation Coordinating Group, based in Oxford. Moreover, rows over numbers are nothing new to the ivory imbroglio. It was to dispel confusion about the impact of ivory poaching on elephant numbers in the 1980s that Douglas-Hamilton and others set up the African Elephant Database at the headquarters of the United Nations Environment Programme (UNEP) in 1986. The figures compiled there suggest that Africa's elephant population crashed from 1.3 million in 1979 to 609 000 in 1989. But—as all elephant conservationists readily acknowledge—these numbers are at best estimates, and since they were first published, they have proved an abiding source of conflict between opposing factions in the ivory debate.

Today, wildlife specialists are becoming increasingly reluctant even to estimate how many elephants are left in Africa. At best, says Cobb, the data are 'spotty'. Trusted figures exist for the elephant populations of Tanzania (52 400) and Kenya (19 058), for example, but the numbers quoted by the governments of Angola and Mozambique are wholly unreliable, he says. For the Sudan and Somalia, moreover, there are no data at all. Last year the World Conservation Union stopped publishing an overall figure for Africa's elephant population. 'It was becoming a joke,' says one of its conservation officers.

The emerging caution over numbers is perhaps only to be expected, given the enormity of the task of monitoring a species that is dispersed across a third of Africa. The scope for error and dispute is magnified by confusion over the elephant's migratory habits and the fact that about 40% of African elephants are forest-dwellers that cannot be seen from the air. Limited resources (aerial surveys cost about $200 per hour), political instability and civil war only make matters worse.

Regardless of their differences over elephant numbers and conservation policy, however, there is one thing on which all wildlife specialists agree: ivory trade or no ivory trade, the African elephant faces a difficult future. Africa's human population is expected to double over the next two decades, putting increasing pressure on the elephant's habitats. Mustafa Tolba, director of the UNEP, issued a bleak statement last month warning that a huge injection of foreign aid 'will be needed to keep herds safe' as growing numbers of people vie for land and resources. The looming habitat crisis is nowhere more evident than in Rwanda.

The human population there is predicted to expand from 7.5 million to 15.6 million over the next 20 years, putting enormous pressure on the 10% of land currently set aside for conservation, and in which the country's one hundred or so surviving elephants are now confined.

And if the elephant loses its habitats, of course, so will Africa's other large mammals. A recent survey of the roan antelope, whose listing in Appendix 2 is to be challenged in Kyoto, concludes reassuringly that the animal is not yet in danger. It adds, however, that if current human demographic and economic trends in Africa go unchecked, the antelope 'and almost all other large African mammals' are likely to be extinct within a century.

In Kyoto, mounting gloom about habitat loss is likely to be seized on by Zimbabwe and its allies as further evidence of the need to resume trade in ivory. Not only would trade generate money for protecting parks against human encroachment, they will argue, but it would increase their economic value to communities that might otherwise destroy them. Supporters of the ivory ban will instead hold up tourism and international aid as the only safe sources of money for protecting habitats.

An emergency blueprint for elephant survival that could form the basis of an international aid package was unveiled last month at an international meeting in Nairobi on elephant conservation. Drawn up by Cobb and his colleagues, the plan comprises 33 separate conservation programmes, one for each African nation with elephants to protect. Its total cost, as estimated by the nations themselves, is $305 million. Uganda, for instance, says it needs $8.8 million to save its remaining 1 910 elephants from extinction, while war-torn Mozambique says that it will need $15.46 million dollars to rebuild its conservation infrastructure if and when peace returns.

Overall, about a quarter of the aid money will be spent on managing and protecting parks, says Cobb, while about 20% will go on research and surveys. Much of the remainder will be spent on rural development, wildlife institutions and public awareness.

Tolba made it clear in Nairobi that it is the industrialized world which will have to foot the bill. His warning was the blunt one which has come to dominate the run-up to the Earth Summit meeting due to be held in Brazil in June: if the rich countries of the North are serious about curing the world's environmental ills, they must back up their prescriptions with the money to buy the medicine.

When it comes to saving Africa's elephants, just how eager will potential donors be to put up the cash when they see Zimbabwe shooting elephants in their thousands? 'Some organisations may find it unpalatable,' admits Cobb, 'but the major donors won't be inhibited.' He believes that implementing the aid package would greatly reduce the need to raise money from ivory.

But why not have both trade and aid? After all, what Zimbabwe and its allies are seeking is not an ivory free-for-all, but tightly regulated trade. 'Too risky' is the response of most conservation organisations, who point out that the mere possibility of a relaxation of the ban has sent the price of ivory on the black market soaring in recent months. There is striking unanimity about what the main obstacle is to controlled trade: verification. As yet there is no easy way to distinguish between poached ivory from say, Kenya and material removed from elephants culled in southern Africa. Moreover, Japan—where vast amounts of illicit ivory were passed off as legal during the 1980s—still has no system for controlling ivory imports.

In an attempt to dispel these worries, Zimbabwe and its allies will highlight in Kyoto recent progress made by South African researchers towards an ivory 'fingerprinting' technique. The method involves measuring the relative abundances in a tusk of the atomic isotopes of carbon, nitrogen and strontium and then matching the resulting isotope 'fingerprint' to one from a tusk of known geographical origins. A similar method can be used for rhino horn (see 'Can we end rhino poaching?', *New Scientist*, 5 October 1991). On paper, the method is a trader's dream. Yet, as supporters of the ivory ban are quick to point out, it is far from ready for commercial application and, even when it is ready, they say, it is likely to be expensive, perhaps as much as $200 per tusk.

Jean-Patrick le Duc, of the CITES secretariat, believes that Zimbabwe has at best a 'small but legitimate' chance of seeing its proposal approved. Yet there is growing concern among wildlife conservationists that the southern African countries must not leave Kyoto empty handed lest they decide to break away from CITES. Already, Zimbabwe believes CITES is out of touch with the views of the majority of conservationists on the policy of 'sustainable utilisation' of wildlife. The smart money, therefore, is on a diplomatic compromise, such as the reopening of trade in hides and meat from elephants culled in southern Africa, but not trade in ivory. There is belief among conservation organisations that this would not put the elephants of eastern and central Africa in jeopardy. 'No one ever shot an African elephant for its hide,' says Simon Lyster, a conservation officer with the World Wide Fund for Nature.

Extract 3.2 describes the outcome of the CITES conference referred to in Extract 3.1.

Extract 3.2 From *New Scientist*, 14 March 1992, p. 11.

African nations defeated over elephant trade

Peter Hadfield, Kyoto

African countries hoping for a relaxation of the ban on ivory trading came away disappointed from the Convention on International Trade in Endangered Species (CITES) in Kyoto. Botswana, Malawi, Zimbabwe and Namibia were forced by international opposition to withdraw proposals that would have allowed the sale of elephant meat and hide and legalised trade of ivory within the four countries.

The African states put forward these watered-down proposals after an initial climbdown last week, when they agreed not to press their case for a resumption of global ivory trading.

Jorgen Thomsen, director of TRAFFIC International, the branch of the World Wide Fund for Nature that monitors trade in animals and animal products, saw the African nations' second defeat as a case of bullying by other countries. 'The decision has given preference to politics over scientific and management principles,' he said.

The issue of ivory trading had threatened to dominate the convention. But passions were also roused over other issues. A call by Sweden to ban fishing of bluefin tuna in the northwestern Atlantic provoked demonstrations by Japanese fishermen outside the conference centre where the CITES meeting was being held. The call also ran into organised opposition inside the centre from Japan, the US, Canada and Morocco.

On Tuesday, the four pro-fishing nations offered to consider reducing their catches by 50 per cent if the Swedes dropped their proposal for a ban. In a backroom deal, Sweden capitulated. The four countries had performed a 'well orchestrated manoeuvre', complained Harry Upton of the American Center for Marine Conservation. 'The biological merits of the proposal weren't discussed.'

Afterwards, the pro-fishing nations were evasive about how and when the 50 per cent reduction would be met. 'The fishermen will have to suffer pain if the 50 per cent cut is implemented, but we believe our goal will be achieved.' said Koji Imamura of the Japanese delegation.

A move by Europe and the US to halt exports of some endangered species of birds caused friction, particularly with Argentina, Guyana, Senegal, Tanzania and Indonesia. The European Community and the US complained that there was little or no monitoring of the trade in birds in their countries of origin. The exporters complained that they were being bullied by the delegates from the industrial North.

The European Community said it would ban the import of species of birds if more than 5 per cent died in transit or quarantine. As many as three million birds are imported into Europe each year, often in appallingly cruel conditions. Around one-third die en route.

The reddest faces in Kyoto last week, however, were not those of anger but embarrassment. As the ivory debate raged in Kyoto, 27 smuggled elephant tusks were discovered in a container of furniture at Kobe, less than 80 kilometres away. The container from South Africa provided ample evidence that the illicit trade in ivory continues in order to fuel the demands of ivory carvers in Japan and elsewhere.

As Extract 3.2 implies, some people saw the conference as a triumph of politics over science. This would certainly be true of the ivory trade controversy if there were only one side to the scientific argument. In fact there are two quite opposite opinions concerning the feasibility of harvesting the African elephant for its ivory. On the one hand there are those scientists and conservation managers, such as Jorgen Thomsen (Extract 3.2), who believe that **sustainable harvesting** is possible and, indeed, the only solution for the African elephant. The term sustainable implies use of a biological resource that does not result in a fall in population size. This group is opposed by those such as Iain Douglas-Hamilton (Extract 3.1) who believe that the low population growth rate of the elephant (coupled with uncertainty about population sizes) provides a strong scientific case for retaining the ban. As was suggested for the blue whale, a low rate of population increase means that only very small numbers of animals may be harvested for resources (e.g. ivory) in any one year. For large-bodied organisms, such as the elephant, even small losses of animals to the ivory-harvester's gun will result in a decline in the populations of that species. For this reason it is unlikely that it will be possible to conserve the African elephant by generating income from the sale of its tusks.

Activity 3.2   *You should spend up to 30 minutes on this activity.*

Read Extract 3.3, which is a letter written to *The Times* by a prominent conservationist in the wake of the CITES meeting. Compare the points made in this letter with your own draft letter in Activity 3.1, which put the counter arguments.

(a) Consider the points made in Pellow's letter, together with points made earlier, and summarize in 100 words or so *your point of view* about this major conservation issue. In particular, do you favour or disapprove of the continuation of the ban in ivory trade, and for what reasons?

(b) Reflect on what factors have led you to the stance expressed in (a). Were you influenced predominantly by the underlying scientific facts, by economic arguments, or more by your own 'feelings'?

Extract 3.3   From *The Times*, 23 March 1992.

'Hollow victory' of ivory trade ban

From Dr Robin Pellew

Sir,

The extended ban on the trade in elephant ivory agreed at the Kyoto conference of the Convention on International Trade in Endangered Species (report, March 11) was a hollow victory for conservation. In reality, this emergency measure is a manifestation of the past failure to effectively manage the species.

Sustainable use should be seen as part of the repertoire of enlightened conservation: trade bans should be the last resort when all else fails. A genuine victory would have been to see sustainable use in effective operation.

The reason why the southern African countries withdrew their proposal for a partial lifting of the ban was the pressure exerted by nations, not least Britain, that exercise no sovereign rights over the management of elephant populations. In countries like Zimbabwe, Botswana and South Africa elephant numbers are increasing, and despite the ban on ivory sales they will continue to be culled to maintain the ecological balance of their habitat.

What these countries sought, and have now been denied, was the opportunity to benefit from their enlightened management policies. By resuming a sustainable trade in skins and ivory under rigorous international controls, they could generate the incentives neces-sary for effective community-based conservation. The opportunities for such creative conservation have now been frustrated.

As stressed by your report, the CITES conference in Japan has produced little of constructive value to secure the future of the African elephant. A compromise to allow a restricted trade in skins but a continued moratorium on ivory has been lost.

It is possible that the alienation of the southern African countries will lead to their withdrawing from CITES and resuming the ivory trade outside the controls of the international Convention. The inevitable consequence will be to exacerbate the threats to the elephant throughout the whole of Africa. The conservation lobby risks scoring an own-goal.

In January, the African states submitted plans to the donor countries for the conservation of their elephant populations. The total cost was in the region of $350 million. In the light of Britain's advocacy of a total ban on all elephant products, its pledge of $1 million towards elephant conservation in Africa is both niggardly and hypocritical.

Yours faithfully,

Robin Pellow (Director),

World Conservation Monitoring Centre, 219 Huntingdon Road, Cambridge.

19 March.

3.3.3 The decline of the black rhinoceros

Unfortunately, despite the clear wording of CITES Appendix I banning trade, evidence from other species shows that it is not always effective. For example, the black rhinoceros (*Diceros bicornis*) has been on CITES Appendix I (a complete trade ban) since 1975 and yet its numbers have crashed to less than 5% of the 1975 value at the time of writing (Table 3.5). These losses are virtually all due to illegal hunting for the horn of the rhinoceros (Table 3.1).

Table 3.5   Changes in the estimates of numbers of black rhinoceros, 1975–1990, whilst receiving CITES Appendix I protection.

year	1975	Late 1970s	1980	1984	1990
numbers of black rhinoceros	80 000	30 000	15 000	9 000	<4 000

Activity 3.3   *You should spend up to 30 minutes on this activity.*

Extract 3.4 illustrates a novel way of protecting the African rhino from poaching—as you know, the horn of the rhino has great 'black market' value.

Read the extract carefully, making brief notes as you go along. Then use these notes as the basis for your answers to (a)–(c), writing in each case a brief list.

(a) Movement of individuals from one site to another (translocation) is an important strategy for the conservation of some species. What disadvantages does this policy have with regard to the desert black rhino?

(b) What precautions and checks have to be made to ensure that the 'dehorning' policy has no adverse effect on desert black rhino individuals?

(b) What precautions and checks have to be made to ensure that the 'dehorning' policy has no adverse effect on desert black rhino individuals?

(c) Provide one example in each case to show how scientific knowledge of the desert black rhino's physiology and habits have helped (i) to shape an effective conservation policy, and (ii) to ensure effective 'de-horning' procedures.

Extract 3.4   From *New Scientist*, 18 November 1989, p. 32.

'Nose jobs' save Namibian rhinos

Sue Armstrong, Johannesburg

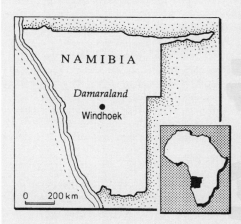

Conservationists working in Damaraland, northwest Namibia, have dehorned desert black rhinos (*Diceros bicornis bicornis*) in an attempt to save them from extinction. They carried out the dehorning, dubbed 'Operation Bicornis', in three months up to June, and pronounce it a success. Although conservationists have been discussing dehorning for several years, this is the first time they have put it into practice in the field.

The desert black rhino is one of four subspecies of African black rhino, and is found throughout Namibia. Earlier this year, poachers began to threaten the species. Rhino horn fetches fabulous prices in the Far East, where it is used in medicines, and in the Yemen, where it is carved into dagger handles.

Dehorning was chosen because it is more practicable than another option—translocation, moving the animals to a place where they can be better protected. Conservation officers are thin on the ground in Damaraland, which is a vast, rugged area, with few people.

Although translocation is widely used in managing game in Africa, conservationists rejected it in Damaraland for several reasons. First, the death rate among rhinos moved is high—about 15 per cent. According to Peter Morkel, the vet with the Game Capture Unit of Namibia's Department of Nature Conservation, the problem does not arise during sedation and transport; only about 2 per cent of rhinos die during this period. Instead, a rhino is most vulnerable immediately after it arrives in its new home—when it is confined in a stockade, or boma, for a few days or weeks—and when it is released into a strange environment.

Translocated rhinos have trouble with their feeding. Rhinos depend on the presence of bacteria in their large gut to ferment their coarse diet. Translocation interrupts their feeding and disturbs the bacteria in the gut, so that the animals quickly become undernourished. Rhinos need a huge amount of energy to survive.

Rhinos suffer considerable stress when they are first released into a strange environment, because they must establish a new territory among unknown rhinos. A rhino has to be taught the intimate details of its home environment by its mother during the first 2 years of its life. It learns, for instance, what it can safely eat and where to find water. Eventually, when its mother moves away to produce a calf elsewhere, the rhino establishes its territory in the area where it has grown up.

For the desert black rhino, the problems associated with translocation would be compounded because it would be moving to a totally different habitat. These rhinos, which live on the semiarid fringe of the Namib desert, have adapted themselves to an environment that is startlingly different from bushveld—the normal habitat of the black rhino.

Until eight years ago, scientists knew little about the desert rhino. Then, Blythe Loutit, a botanical illustrator who had stumbled across their giant footprints in the sand near Damaraland's Skeleton Coast, started a study of what they ate. Loutit found that the desert black rhino is an opportunistic feeder which will even eat grass when the food is available.

This is a habit unheard of among black rhinos of the bushveld, where they are browsers, mainly of leaves. One of the desert rhino's favourite foods is the *Welwitschia mirabilis*, an extremely primitive relative of the conifer that is unique to the Namib desert.

The poor diet of the desert black rhino means that when it is being moved, it has less stored energy to fall back on during the period of interrupted feeding. Also, says Morkel, translocation lengthens the time it takes for the bacteria in the gut to adapt to a new diet.

Operation Bicornis has in fact involved the translocation of a few animals, with tragic results for some. A cow that was translocated with her small calf fell to her death over a cliff recently, and a young bull has also died from eating an unfamiliar, poisonous plant.

The dehorning process itself involved far less risk, and the team lost no rhinos. They darted the animals from a helicopter, using neuroleptic anaesthesia. This is a mixture of M99, the semisynthetic opioid etorphine hydrochloride, which immobilises the animals, and azaperone, a sedative that reduces the 'narcotic excitement' that is a side effect of M99. Morkel also added the spreading agent hyaluronidase to the syringe to ensure that the rhinos absorbed the other two drugs.

Timing is critical in this procedure. If an animal makes a short run after darting, this helps to circulate the drug round the body. If it makes a long run before collapsing, this may speed up the physiological processes to a dangerous degree. Because M99 is a powerful respiratory depressant, Morkel always administers a small dose of respiratory stimulant, doxapram hydrochloride, as soon as he reaches the animal. This bridges the time during which the animal is in so-called 'oxygen debt' because it has been running.

Morkel checks the heart rate and temperature immediately after capturing a rhino. If an animal's temperature is above what he considers the critical level of 39 °C, he will abandon the dehorning and give the antidote. Throughout the operation, assistants throw water over the rhino to prevent it overheating in the sun.

After removing the tranquillising dart, the vet squirts an antibiotic into the wound. This is important because rhinos can develop abscesses which tend to fester under their thick skin. Also, the dart can damage the muscle slightly because it is fitted with an explosive internal charge which delivers the drug at high speed. Morkel also administers benzyl penicillin, an antibiotic, to prevent infection in any small wounds that may be caused during the operation.

Workers cut off the horn about 6.5 centimetres above skin level, which is just above the quick. Once they have clipped the stump and filed it smooth, they paint it with mildly antiseptic Stockholm Tar in case there are any small abrasions. Then a vet gives the antidote M50-50 (diprenorphine hydrochloride). In just over a minute, the animal is back on its feet.

Since the end of the dehorning operations, game guards have camped out in the desert. Supervised by Loutit, they have monitored the animals involved to see if hornlessness has affected their social interaction, their ability to defend themselves against each other and predators, or their feeding habits. 'Absolutely no ill effects have been observed so far,' says Loutit.

In the past few months, two calves have been born to mothers with 'nose jobs', leading the team to believe that females are no less attractive to males, despite their radical surgery. Loutit also says that there is no more poaching in Damaraland. Instead, the poachers have moved northwards to the vast game region of Etosha.

These stories of decline among the blue whale, African elephant and black rhinoceros following resource exploitation demonstrate that we have to look very carefully at biological resources as a reason for conservation. Conserving a species in order to harvest its resources may have an effect that is just the opposite of that desired. As you have seen, some people argue that populations can be harvested sustainably, that the resource can be removed without affecting the size of the population. This is certainly possible in theory but there are many practical difficulties. Unfortunately, the alternative of a complete trade ban can also be, as we have seen, unsuccessful.

Issues of sustainable harvesting have also come to the fore in the exploitation of the tropical moist forests, a subject which is discussed in the next section.

3.3.4 Harvesting the tropical forests

In Chapter 2 we learnt about the species richness of the tropical moist forests. Although we concentrated on insect species, many other animal and plant groups have their highest numbers of species in these forests. Not least amongst these are the trees which form the fabric of the forest and which are also being lost at a rapid rate (Table 2.2). There may be 200 different tree species in a 1-hectare ($100\,\text{m} \times 100\,\text{m}$) area. This compares with perhaps ten species in an equivalent area of temperate forest.

Harvesting the forest does not necessarily mean cutting down the trees. Many tree species have been used by indigenous peoples for thousands of years, often in ways which do not kill the plant. It is only in recent years that we in the 'developed' world have come to appreciate the full extent of this use. An important source of information about the uses of tropical plants has come from the work of ethnobotanists, who study the taxonomy of plants (see Box 6.1, p.86) and talk to local people to find out how they use particular plant species. For example, Dr Brian Boom has shown the extent of biological resource use by four indigenous Amazonian groups, demonstrating that they use between 49% and 79% of tree species in their area.

Extract 3.5 reproduces an article by Linda Fellows that places the present day loss of primary rainforest in a broader, global context. In particular, Fellows attempts to estimate the economic costs of continued deforestation in terms of the loss of plant-derived drugs.

Activity 3.4   *You should spend up to 1 hour on this activity.*

Read Extract 3.5, following whatever reading strategy helps you to identify the major features of the argument most easily. Note the way in which relevant publications are referred to in the text and listed at the end of the paper. Then answer questions (a)–(f), some of which relate to the broader issues covered in the extract. Note that 'phytochemicals' are plant-based chemicals and 'biodiversity' refers to the range of plant and animal species (considered in detail in Chapter 6).

(a) In the author's view, why has 'the global crisis' continued to worsen despite '20 years of expert analysis, conferences, and resolution'?

(b) In what respects does Fellows' categorization of the value of plants go further than the approach adopted in Section 3.3, which simply lists 'biological resources'?

(c) How do the estimates given in Extract 3.5 for (i) the proportion of species within the tropical forests, and (ii) rates of deforestation compare with estimates given earlier in Chapter 2. (Note for (ii) that $1\,\text{km}^2 = 100\,\text{hectares}$.)

(d) Why might the disturbingly high estimate of deaths from hunger in Africa over the next 20 years represent too pessimistic a view of future developments?

(e) Summarize, in about 100 words, the procedures followed by Peter Principe (quoted by Fellows) to quantify the economic effects for medicine of species loss.

(f) Finally, put the information in the article to use by supposing that you have 60 seconds of radio time to put a case against continued destruction of the tropical rainforest. Use facts from Extract 3.5 where possible, but think of ways of maximizing their impact on your audience.

Extract 3.5   From *The Lancet*, **339**, 30 May 1992, pp. 1330–1333.

What are the forests worth?

Linda Fellows

In 1972, the Canadian, Maurice Strong, organised a world environment conference in Stockholm at which over-population, vegetation destruction, and pollution were identified as serious threats to our planet and consequently to the human enterprise.[1] The following year, at another Stockholm conference, Population and the Environment, it was acknowledged that there are ultimate limits to economic growth, but that we remain almost totally ignorant about the factors that determine such limits, the seriousness of the disruption to ecosystems caused by human exploitation of natural resources, the type of technological intervention needed to extend these limits, and their potential to do so. Two decades later, after an almost complete failure of society to come to grips with this dilemma, and with rapidly worsening emissions of 'greenhouse' gases such as CO_2, Strong is behind next week's much-heralded Earth Summit, as Secretary General of the UN Conference on Environment and Development in Rio de Janeiro. World leaders will be asked to sign an 'Earth Charter' of environmental and economic principles that would pave the way to fundamental changes in world economic systems (including a 'polluter pays' principle), believed by many to be essential to preserve civilisation.

Why has the global crisis continued to worsen despite 20 years of expert analysis, conferences, and resolutions? Under traditional economic rules, change has been neither economically viable nor politically expedient, and the burning of fossil fuels, the destruction of forests, and the release of industrial pollutants has been justified in the short term. Additionally, the trade in plants has been driven by market prices, and not by an appreciation of the true economic value of a species or of species diversity. The full economic value of a plant species has two elements: the *use* value, which includes the current and future utilitarian value of the species, and the *non-use* value, which is the vicarious value placed by individuals on the continued existence of a species (e.g. a rare orchid). *Use* values can be *direct* (local consumption, use in plant breeding or medicine, tourist amenity), *indirect* (e.g. through their contribution to essential ecological processes such as nutrient recycling, watershed protection, and air pollution reduction), and *optional* (the possibility that a species might have some future use in any of these categories). Usually the monetary value of plants encompasses only the direct market value of those that are traded and not any of the non-market prices nor any of the indirect values that might be attributed to them, so they are inevitably underestimates of their true monetary worth.[2]

The greatest diversity of plant species is found in the tropical forests, which have shrunk from 15–16 million km^2 in 1940 to 8 million km^2 (14% of the world land surface) today.[2,3] They are the habitats of 60% of known plant species. Of the two main types of forest (dry and moist), the tropical moist forests (TMFs), which make up only 5–7% of the land surface, contain more than half the species of the entire biosphere. Large areas of TMFs are concentrated in a few developing countries—notably Brazil, Indonesia, Cameroon, Gabon, and the Congo—where population growth has led to an acceleration of the rate of land clearance, mostly through small-scale farming. 75 000 km^2 of rainforest and 38 000 km^2 of other forest types are now lost annually, and if the trend continues, the rainforests will be completely lost within 30 years.

The human population (4.4 billion in 1980) is on course to reach 7.7 billion by 2020.[4,5] We already consume 40% of the net products of photosynthesis of the globe. The acceleration of Third World population growth since the 1939–45 war, associated with a rapid reduction in mortality rates, has slowed down in Latin America since the 1960s. However, growth has remained high in other areas, especially sub-Saharan Africa, where people are heavily dependent on agriculture and children are regarded as having a high economic value. That nearly half the population is under 15 years old portends a further population explosion. Although the AIDS pandemic has led some people to ask whether it will reverse this trend, one calculation suggests that even if the current highest infection rate (in Uganda) were applied to the whole of Africa, the population growth rate would only fall from 3% to 1.8%, which remains above the current world average of 1.7%. The agricultural land area of the world (estimated at 7.70 million km^2 in the early 1980s) is expected to grow by 11% to reach 8.53 million km^2 by the turn of the century, mostly as a result of forest conversion.

Nonetheless, since 1980, the population increase has outstripped the global increase in food production (1.4% per year). In particular, this difference is seen in 27 out of 39 countries in sub-Saharan Africa.[5] In the drier lands there, as in the Middle East and north-west Asia, overgrazing, firewood collection, and land overuse are leading to soil depletion and the creation of more deserts. If present trends continue, Africa will be able to feed only 40% of its population by 2025. The number of deaths from hunger could increase five-fold to around 1 billion over the next 20 years.

The loss of plant life goes hand in hand with the loss of animal and microbial life, leading to a breakdown of ecological processes and life support systems. The Earth Summit will have to consider the long-term implications of two distinct aspects of this loss—loss of forest areas per se, with the attendant effects on climate, and loss of biodiversity. Despite scientific uncertainty (which habitats and genes are being lost) and economic uncertainty (lack of knowledge of future trends and patterns of income, preferences, and technologies) there is one irrefutable fact: extinction is final. It may be inevitable that some extinction be traded for economic development: the question we must answer now is how much extinction can we allow today while still retaining the options of a plant gene pool that will meet the unknown needs of our descendants? In other words, we must place a value on the unknown. To convince politicians that sacrifices today are justified for the sake of economic benefits tomorrow, one has to put a price tag on the unknown.

The use of plants in medicine is one aspect of plant exploitation for which there are data that can be used to help forecast future financial benefits forfeited when biodiversity is lost today. Plants have always had an important role in medicine and public health.[6] In developing countries, more than 80% of the population depends upon traditional plant-based medicine,[7] and even in the USA, for example, 25% of prescription drugs are still based on phytochemicals (from only 40 species). US researcher Peter Principe (ref. 8 and personal communication) has courageously used existing data to examine the market value of plant-based chemicals in three ways. First, he estimates the present market value of plant-based prescriptions. Second, he estimates the potential foregone (i.e. never realised) market value of drugs that will not be discovered because species will have become extinct; this is a speculative future value of undiscovered plant-based pharmaceuticals. Finally, he estimates the present value of the foregone market value of plant-based drugs that will not be marketed—an amount that can be taken to indicate what might be a reasonable minimum expenditure today to preserve the plants that would provide the undiscovered drugs of the future.

Using available commercial data, Principe estimates that the 1990 retail value of plant-based drugs in the USA is $15.5 billion. On the assumption that prescriptions in 1990 were still based on 40 plant species, the average contribution per species was a little under $390 million. He cites a consensus of drug development professionals that a reasonable estimate of the likelihood that any given plant will yield a marketable prescription drug is in the range 1 in 1000 to 1 in 10000, and for the purposes of calculating his estimates of foregone value he uses the mid-point, 5 in 10000 or 1 in 2000.

Of the estimated 250 000 known plant species, about 25% will be extinct by the year 2050. If we assume that the rate of loss will be constant between 1991 and 2050, the annual loss will be 1059 species, of which about 30 might yield marketable drugs (about 1 every two years). The foregone benefit in the first year can thus be estimated to be about $200 million, increasing every year thereafter by the same amount, reaching $11–12 billion (1990 dollars) by 2050. To estimate the present value of this foregone benefit, Principe assumes a 5% discount rate, which suggests that this amount is today worth over $3.5 billion. This value only refers to retail sales, and takes no account of other economic gains, such as lives saved or extended and ecosystem benefits (contribution to maintenance of the complex web of ecological processes). Using the best available data on the value of a life (US citizen) and the anti-cancer benefits of plant-based drugs, he estimates that the current value of foregone benefits from anti-cancer uses alone might be as high as $7 thousand billion. He emphasises that these estimates are unlikely to be useful in making specific public policy decisions, but show the potential magnitude of the benefits and define areas in which methods for better quantification of the benefits of ecosystems can be further developed.

Principe's estimate of $3.5 billion reflects the minimum amount the developed world must spend now to protect its future interests (contrast this with the estimated $750 billion now spent annually on arms[9]), but it is equally important for developing countries that plant life be preserved. Investment in collaborative conservation programmes has already begun in the form of grants and aid packages, but this needs to be increased. Revenue could theoretically be diverted to such projects in several ways. Myers[3] suggested a direct tax on tropical products sold in developed countries. Alternatively, increased export revenue could be generated. Recently there have been efforts to 'farm' both timber and non-timber forest products for export in such a way that conservation does not compromise future production. Pearce[10] suggests that government interference has been responsible for much past non-sustainable timber extraction and that, if left to market forces, natural management schemes based on selective cutting with natural regeneration would ensure supplies. Non-timber forest products are now important sources of revenue. For example, the value of such exports from Indonesia reached $238 million in 1987.[10]

Investment by chemical companies in return for exclusive rights to investigate the chemicals of tropical forest plants (more than 95% of which have never been subject to chemical scrutiny) may also assist conservation if not preservation. The loss of chemical structures before they can be evaluated has been likened to the loss of the great libraries of Alexandria, but until recently interest in plants by the pharmaceutical and pesticide industry was slight. In 1980, not one US company admitted to doing research into higher plants. This situation has now changed dramatically. By 1990, 107 US companies (223 world wide) were involved in plant research with several clinical trials in progress.[11] One reason for this sudden reversal of attitude is the commercial success of new plant-derived drugs, e.g. the anti-cancer drugs vincristine and vinblastine derived from the rosy periwinkle (*Catharanthus roseus*) (Eli Lilly, retail value $100 million in 1985), and etoposide, derived from a compound in the mayapple (*Podophyllum peltatum*) and worth about $15 million in 1989. The US company Merck has recently invested $1 million over two years in a project in Costa Rica, which has 11 000 plant species—5.7% of the world's total. 10% of the money will go immediately to conservation and the remainder will fund the training of local taxonomists. Royalties from the sale of any product arising from the programme will be shared between Merck and Costa Rica although the proportion that each will receive is undisclosed (L. Corporale, personal communication). It remains to be seen whether this type of arrangement will be repeated by other pharmaceutical companies. Principe's calculations might indicate that Merck's investment was relatively low. Companies might reply that prospecting for new drugs is expensive, with the average cost of getting a new drug to market exceeding $200 million (Aylward, personal communication).

Lately there has been much speculation about what will happen to world economies when supplies of fossil fuels are exhausted. So far, discovery of new sources has more than kept pace with demand and at present there is a glut, so much so that it now seems likely that the value of plants as a 'sink' for CO_2 emissions will soon be regarded as a scarcer and more important resource than the fuels themselves.[12] Forest destruction leads to release of CO_2 which contributes an estimated 1–3 billion tonnes of carbon annually into the atmosphere. This quantity is overshadowed by the release of 5–6 billion tonnes of carbon annually as a result of the combustion of fossil fuels, mostly by the industrialised nations, which, it is feared, is leading to the warming of middle and high latitudes in both hemispheres. Woodwell[13] predicts that the changes will be rapid enough to exceed the capacity of existing forests to migrate or adapt. Forest trees will die at the warmer and drier limits more rapidly than they can be regenerated in more favourable areas, and the decay of organic matter will itself release further CO_2, exacerbating the problem. A vigorous reforestation programme could theoretically remove about 1 billion tonnes of carbon from the atmosphere for each 2 million km^2 of land replanted. However, Friends of the Earth suggest that reforestation on a large scale is unrealistic and would reduce biodiversity through damage to wildlife habitats, degrade soils, and lead to the forced resettlement of subsistence farmers.[14] There seems to be no alternative to reducing CO_2 emissions and halting forest destruction.

On Maurice Strong's agenda for the Earth Summit is the principle that the industrialised world must pay inter alia for taking up more than its fair share of the earth's ability to absorb CO_2. Interviewed for *New Scientist*,[1] he said that his programme would not signal the end of economic growth, but would bring about massive gains in the efficiency with which natural resources are used; he cited the industrial success of Japan, allegedly one of the most efficient users of energy. Strong believes that the real barriers to a sustainable world economy are not related to finance or technology, but to attitude and political will. Whether the summit accepts his agenda or not, he is confident that the world will be shocked into realising what needs to be done.

I thank Mr Bruce Aylward, Ms Jocelynne Henry, Mr Peter Principe for their help in the preparation of this article.

References

1 MacKenzie, D. (1991) Strong words to save the planet, *New Scientist*, 10 August, p. 17.

2 Flint, M. (1991) *Biological Diversity and Developing Countries: Issues and Options*, Overseas Development Administration publication.

3 Myers, N. (1989) The future of forests, in Friday, L. and Laskey, R. (eds) *The Fragile Environment*, Cambridge University Press, pp. 22–40.

4 Anon (1991) Parliamentary Office of Science and Technology Briefing Note 25, World Population, London: POST.

5 Bilsborrow, R. E. and Okoth-Ogendo, H. W. O. (1992) Population driven changes in land-use in developing countries, *Ambio*, **21**, pp. 37–45.

6 Akerele, O., Heywood, V. and Synge, H. (eds) (1991) The conservation of medicinal plants. *Proceedings of a Conference 21–27 March 1988, Chiang Mai, Thailand*, Cambridge University Press.

7 Farnsworth, N. R. and Soejarto, D. D. (1985) Potential consequences of plant extinction in the United States on the current and future availability of prescription drugs, *Economic Botany*, **39**, pp. 231–40.

8 Principe, P. (1989) The economic significance of plants and their constituents as drugs, in Wagner, H., Hikino, H. and Farnsworth, N. R. (eds) *Economic and Medicinal Plant Research*, **3**, Academic Press.

9 Russell, P. (1992) *The White Hole in Time: Our Future Evolution and the Meaning of Now*, Aquarian Press.

10 Pearce, D. W. (1991) An economic approach to saving the tropical forests, *London Environmental Economics Centre Paper 90–06*, London LEEC.

11 Fellows, L. E. (1992) Pharmaceuticals from traditional medicinal plants and other species: future prospects, in Coombes, J. D. (ed.) *New Drugs from Natural Sources. International Business Communication Technical Series*, pp. 95–102.

12 Patterson, W. (1991) Are we throwing away the planet's future? *New Scientist*, 16 November, p. 8.

13 Woodwell, G. M. (1989) The warming of the industrialised middle latitudes 1985–2050: causes and consequences. *Climatic Change*, **15**, pp. 31–50.

14 Friends of the Earth (1992) *Deserts of Trees*, Friends of the Earth.

3.4 Conclusion

In this chapter we have considered the assumption made in Chapters 1 and 2 that conservation is intrinsically a good thing. First, it is easy to argue that biological conservation is necessary for selfish (human) reasons, because species represent sources of food, medicine or ornamental products. However, in our desire to attain these products, it is all too easy to overexploit plant or animal populations. Second, particular plants, animals and their habitats have a value beyond pure economic return. They represent symbols of culture and beauty or sources of knowledge. Perhaps here abuse of such species is reduced, although we still feel the urge to collect rather than simply observe. At least this second motivation to conserve is moving closer to an unselfish ideal where plant and animal species are conserved for *their* sake rather than for *ours*.

Summary of Chapter 3

1 Reasons for stopping the losses of species and habitats include the aesthetic qualities of the organisms and their habitats, the knowledge gained from species-rich habitats, and uses of the organisms as biological resources.

2 There is a huge variety of uses of animals and plants, many of which require the individual to be killed. This has the potential to reduce population size and therefore increase the likelihood of species extinction.

3 The link between species extinction and resource use is seen most clearly in large bodied animals and plants, such as the African elephant, the blue whale, and tropical forest trees.

4   It is possible to calculate the cost of species extinction in terms of the loss of potential and actual resources. This calculation has been attempted with reference to the medicinal uses of tropical plants, revealing that deforestation may cost 200 million US dollars per year.

Activity 3.5   *You should spend up to 15 minutes on this activity.*

This activity is designed to make you look beyond the cold facts on uses of animals presented in this chapter.

What is your personal opinion on the uses of animals described in this chapter? Attempt to summarize it in no more than 100 words.

I expect there will be two extremes of reaction with others left somewhere in the middle. At one extreme, there will be those of you who feel that no animal use which involves killing the animal can ever be justified. If you fall into this category then you should consider how you would convey this message to a group of indigenous peoples who may have been killing animals for thousands of years. For those of you who feel that any use of animals is acceptable, how would you deal with the criticism that you are endangering a species such as the African elephant as a result of harvesting for a resource?

---

4 Monitoring of endangered species

The most fundamental and natural division of the world's flora and fauna is into different species. This is also the biological unit which is most often described as in need of conservation, whether it be the giant panda (*Ailuropoda melanoleuca*), the blue whale (*Balaenoptera musculus*) or the lady's slipper orchid (*Cypripedium calceolus*). Species are divided up into populations (Section 2.1.1), and much of this chapter will deal with assessing the size of populations. You will recall from Chapter 2 that a population was defined as those individuals of a species that live close to each other and so are likely to interbreed.

Conserving a species depends upon locating the populations and then assessing the numbers of individuals in those populations. Thereafter, the monitoring of the change in this population size with time is a necessary prerequisite for determining the extent to which those populations require the types of protection and/or management strategies that will be examined in more detail in Chapter 5. We look first at the process of locating populations and assessing population size in Sections 4.1 and 4.2.

4.1 Getting started

Identification of an endangered species is not a trivial task. Information on some species is so limited that it is impossible to tell if they are threatened: indeed, it is likely that there are many species, particularly in the tropics, whose existence is unknown (Section 2.2.1). On a more positive note, there is now accurate, detailed information available for many plants, vertebrates and some insects, e.g. butterflies, which allows rare and possibly endangered species to be identified. This is particularly true in Britain and parts of North America and mainland Europe, where there is a long tradition of studying ecology and natural history.

The most basic information available on an endangered species is its geographic range or spatial distribution. Such information is usually in the form of presence/absence data within grid squares of a certain size. Figure 4.1 shows the change in the distribution of the early spider orchid (*Ophrys sphegodes*) in Great Britain; Plate 4.1 shows the individual plant. The data in Figure 4.1 show whether the plant was present or absent within 10 km × 10 km squares, recorded over three periods of time. A dot, signifying the presence of the species within that square, may represent just one plant or a large population of plants. Whilst the type of information presented in Figure 4.1 is helpful in describing the geographic range of the early spider orchid, it says nothing about the abundance of the plant within any one grid square. A detailed population study examining individual plants is needed for this, as outlined in Section 4.2.

Question 4.1 Describe from Figure 4.1 how the geographic range of the early spider orchid in Great Britain has changed over the last 60 years.

The geographic range and presence/absence data are useful in two ways when embarking on a detailed population study. First, they indicate whether a species has a limited and/or declining range (if recorded over several years) and therefore suggest candi-

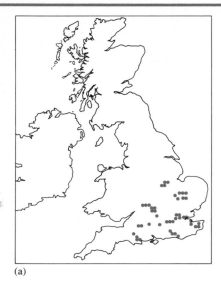

(a)   (b)   (c)

Figure 4.1 Distribution of the early spider orchid (*Ophrys sphegodes*) in Great Britain, (a) pre-1930, (b) between 1930 and 1974, and (c) after 1975, based on a survey of 10km × 10km squares.

dates in need of conservation, such as the early spider orchid. Second, they can help locate ideal sites for detailed population studies. For example, if the range of a species appears to be contracting, it may be helpful to study a site at the edge of the species range where the factors reducing its range might be expected to be most pronounced. In fact, the choice of site for detailed population studies is often determined by more pragmatic reasons: studies may need to be undertaken over long periods of time and involve expensive equipment, so therefore site security is important; sites may also be chosen for ease of access, or because the history of the site is well known.

4.2 Collecting data on population size

Population size can be measured as the number of individuals of one species living in a particular area, e.g. 1km². In this section, a study of the population of early spider orchids in southern England will be described in detail. Reasons why orchid species might be suitable candidates for conservation were identified in Section 3.1. The early spider orchid has been highlighted as a species with a declining range whose populations are worth studying (Figure 4.1).

In order to understand the reasons for the early spider orchid's decline in Great Britain, a detailed population study was begun in 1975 at a site on the chalk downs in Sussex. This work, which continues into the 1990s, has been undertaken by Dr Mike Hutchings and his colleagues from the University of Sussex. Each year during April and May an assessment of the population size is made by counting the number of flowering and non-flowering early spider orchid plants within a 20m × 20m permanent plot. This is a laborious process, in which the plants (Plate 4.1), which are often tiny, are located amongst grasses and other plants, and their position recorded to the nearest 0.5cm. This record of position is kept so that the same individual plant can be relocated, if present, in subsequent years.

This highly detailed exercise monitoring the change in size of the plant population is also intended to shed light on the loss of the plant in other parts of Britain. One result of the study is shown in Figure 4.2, which depicts the number of flowering plants over a 10-year period within the 20m × 20m plot.

Question 4.2 Briefly describe the change with time in the number of flowering early spider orchids, shown in Figure 4.2.

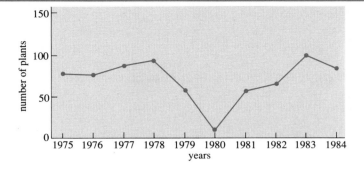

Figure 4.2 The number of early spider orchid plants observed flowering in the Sussex site each year, from 1975 to 1984.

The method of recording the positions of plants and finding them again in subsequent years had a bonus which only became apparent after several years study. Some individual plants were found to have 'disappeared' in one year only to re-emerge at roughly the same spot in the following or subsequent years (Figure 4.3). It was discovered that these plants were dormant during their 'hidden' years, remaining underground as a pair of rounded tubers with a few fleshy roots.

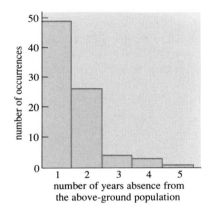

Figure 4.3 The lengths of dormant periods observed in the early spider orchid population in the Sussex site, from 1975 to 1984.

Question 4.3 What can be inferred from Figure 4.3 about the minimum length of time for a project to monitor the survival of the early spider orchid?

The success of this project depends not only on counting the number of individual plants, but also on measuring other variables which may affect the population. These include climatic variables such as rainfall: changing weather patterns might be one explanation for the declining geographic range or for the marked reduction in flowering plants in 1980 (Figure 4.2). It is therefore important to measure the rainfall (for example) at the site and attempt to assess its effect on the population. However, the effect of rainfall and other climatic variables on population change is a very wide-ranging and difficult topic, beyond the scope of this book.

4.2.1 Can we count all the individuals in a population?

The early spider orchid example has shown that, even for apparently conspicuous and sessile organisms such as flowering plants, it can be very difficult to count *all* the individuals of a particular species in a study area.

▷   What two problems do you envisage in attempting to count *all* the individuals in a population?

▶ First, the population may exist over a very large area, so there is the straightforward problem of effort and time. Second, the individuals may be very small and/or hidden and/or mobile. As with the early spider orchid, not all organisms sit above ground every year and wait to be counted! Indeed, even in a population with very large immobile individuals, such as the pedunculate oak (*Quercus robur*), there will be small inconspicuous individuals, such as viable acorns or newly emerged seedlings.

The solution to these problems is to **sample** the population, counting individuals or measuring the population size in some other way in a small area, e.g. 20 m × 20 m for the early spider orchid, and then to extrapolate to the whole population. This provides an *estimate* of the size of a population in the absence of an absolute count of the individuals in the whole population. Ecology has provided conservation workers with a large number of different sampling techniques. Three of these techniques—counting individuals, indirect methods (e.g. counting droppings), and using traps—are described in Sections 4.2.2–4.2.4, along with examples of their application.

4.2.2 Sampling by counting individuals

For many mobile animals, direct observation and recording of individuals is the best method of sampling. In Britain, the Butterfly Monitoring Scheme uses a 'walk-and-count' method to assess the size of butterfly populations at different places in the country (about 80 sites were covered in 1989). A recorder follows the same walk, usually once a week, from the beginning of April until the end of September (26 recording weeks), noting the number of adult butterflies of each species seen. The route for the walk is chosen to cover a range of habitats where adult butterflies are known to fly. The recorder walks at a uniform pace recording all butterflies within 5 metres of them. All but two butterfly species in Britain can be distinguished in flight.

This sampling system is different from those outlined in the following two sections in that it provides an estimate of the *relative* size of different populations, for example there are four times as many individuals in one population compared to another, and of the relative changes in the size of one population with time. We cannot use the data to estimate the (unknown) absolute population size of a species in any one year. Data for two butterfly species from an area of chalk grassland on the South Downs in Sussex are given in Table 4.1.

Table 4.1 The total number of individuals of two butterfly species seen over a 26-week period at a National Nature Reserve in southern England. The chalkhill blue (*Lysandra coridon*), as the name suggests, is characteristic of chalk and other limestone grassland, and is restricted to southern England but is widespread in central mainland Europe. The marbled white (*Melanargia galathea*) has a similar distribution to the chalkhill blue in Britain but occurs further south in Europe. The marbled white also occurs over a wider range of grassland types than the chalkhill blue.

Year	chalkhill blue	marbled white
1978	1 835	52
1979	2 720	40
1980	1 240	17
1981	585	62
1982	1 085	101
1983	1 530	297
1984	3 016	482
1985	2 540	683
1986	4 514	1 248
1987	2 790	471

▷ Quantify the *relative* size of the chalkhill blue butterfly population in 1980 compared with 1981.

▶ The answer is found by dividing the number in 1980 (1 240) by the number in 1981 (585): 1 240/585 = 2.1. Therefore, based on the numbers seen, the chalkhill blue population in 1980 was roughly twice as large as that in 1981.

▷ Quantify the *relative* size of the chalkhill blue population in 1987 compared to the size of the marbled white population.

▶ In 1987, 2 790 chalkhill blue butterflies were seen, compared to 471 marbled white butterflies. Therefore, the relative size of the chalkhill blue population compared to the marbled white was 2790/471 = 5.9, i.e. in 1987 the population of chalkhill blue butterflies was nearly six times larger than the population of marbled white butterflies.

There are a number of potential problems with the walk-and-count sampling method, as the following example illustrates. Suppose you were set the task of comparing numbers of butterflies of a variety of species in one site. A sensible strategy might be to walk-and-count at the same time each day, but the different species may fly at different times of day or perhaps be differently affected by certain weather conditions. It may also be that one butterfly species is more easily seen than others, so that their recorded relative population size may not reflect their true population size at that site. Comparing butterfly counts at different sites may be even more problematic.

Activity 4.1   *You should spend up to 30 minutes on this activity.*

It is often much easier to see any particular trends or anomalies in the data when they are expressed in diagrammatic form rather than in a table of numbers such as Table 4.1.

(a) Note down *three* graphs you could plot using the data in Table 4.1.

(b) For what reasons would you choose to plot the data in each of these three ways, i.e. what trends (if present) would you hope to reveal?

(c) Plot the three graphs, making sure you label the axes, include the scales, and provide titles. Do your graphs reveal any interesting trends in the data?

4.2.3 Sampling by indirect methods

An alternative to the direct counting of animals is the collection of evidence of their activities.

▷   What type of evidence of animal activity might provide information on the abundance of those animals?

▶   Faecal pellets, bark scraping or leaf chewing can all provide an indirect estimate of the abundance of the animals that made or caused them.

It is a perverse fact that the largest land animal in the world, the African elephant (*Loxodonta africana*), is one whose populations sometimes need to be sampled indirectly, by counting the dung of the animal to produce estimates of population size.

▷   Elephants can also be counted from the air. What are the disadvantages of this method?

▶   Remember from Box 1 in Extract 3.1 that such methods are expensive and depend upon the animals being in open habitats such as grassland. It has also been described as being 'very boring, tedious and tiring'!

In forest areas, sampling often has to be undertaken by recording the amount of dung. This method has been applied to other endangered species, such as the giant panda in bamboo forests in China. In addition to using dung counts as estimates of population size, examination of the contents of dung may be used to determine the diet of animals.

Two important pieces of information are required when estimating elephant numbers based on the number of droppings. First, the number of droppings produced per elephant per day, which will vary with the age of the elephant and between seasons. For example, for bull elephants the defaecation rate varies from 31 per animal per day in the early and middle rainy seasons to about 12 per day in the dry season. The second piece of information required is the number of days over which dung has accumulated.

If elephants stay in one place for a long time they may defaecate repeatedly in that area. If all this dung were counted then there would be an *over*estimate of the number of elephants present. A knowledge of the time over which dung has accumulated makes it possible to correct for this overestimate.

Knowing the defaecation rate per elephant per day (R), the number of days over which droppings have accumulated (A), (taking into account decomposition rates, which vary throughout the year), and the number of (estimated) droppings in the whole area (D), a formula can be derived to estimate the number of elephants (N), in the whole area:

$$N = D/(R \times A) \tag{4.1}$$

▷   Why is it possible only to *estimate* the number of droppings produced by elephants?

▶   The number of droppings can only be estimated because it is simply not possible to count all the dung in, say, the area of a national park. The amount of dung in the larger area is therefore estimated from counts in smaller areas.

Question 4.4   In a study in the Kasungu National Park, Malawi, D was estimated as 8 267 000; R was measured as 17 droppings per elephant per day, and A was 188 days.

(a) Using these values, calculate the value of N, the estimated number of elephants in the park.

(b) Which of the values given above are estimates?

(c) How could you cross-check the value of N given by the formula?

This method of estimating population size raises important questions about the reliability of particular estimates—a crucial factor when discussing contentious issues such as the ivory trade (Extracts 3.1 and 3.2).

4.2.4 Sampling using traps

The key to successfully estimating the size of animal populations in any habitat is to know something of the ecology and behaviour of the individual animals. For example, with small mammals such as mice, some knowledge of their feeding preferences and patterns of movement allows traps to be positioned correctly and baited with something they like eating. Simple records of captures will provide some information on the variety of species present and the relative sizes of the populations. However, the *best* estimates of population size come from capturing animals, marking them, releasing them, and then recapturing a proportion of them at a later time. These **mark–release–recapture methods** provide data which allow an estimate to be made of the size of a population. If each animal is given a unique mark (e.g. a numbered ear tag), the distance an animal moves (presuming it is caught in different traps) can also be estimated. The basic steps in the method are outlined here:

1   Animals are caught in traps, or by some other method, over a short period of time, e.g. a single night.

2   All these animals are marked in some way and then released. The number of caught and marked animals is recorded. It is important that neither the mark nor the trapping affect the behaviour or survival of the animal. Although this is an assumption of mark–release–recapture techniques, it is not always satisfied.

3   Traps are reset, and some animals are recaptured, perhaps on the night following marking and release. Two pieces of information are recorded: the total number of captures; and the number of recaptured animals, i.e. those marked on the first trapping occasion.

Knowing the proportion of *re*captured animals allows an estimate to be made of the total population size. Suppose that 25 animals are caught on the first occasion. These are marked and released. On the second occasion 30 animals are caught of which 10 are marked from the first sample. Therefore, 10/30 or one-third of the second sample are *re*captures. We know that 25 animals were originally marked. If they had mixed back evenly into the total population then we would expect that the fraction of marked individuals in the second sample (one-third) should be equal to the fraction of marked individuals in the total population. Therefore if the total population is *T*, then $25/T = 1/3$, so $T = 3 \times 25 = 75$ individuals. This is the basis of all mark–release–recapture techniques.

Following this argument an equation can be derived for the total number of individuals (*T*) in a population:

number of individuals caught and marked on first occasion = N_1,

total number of individuals caught on second occasion = N_2,

number of marked individuals captured on second occasion = M_2,

we expect $\dfrac{N_1}{T} = \dfrac{M_2}{N_2}$, therefore

$$T = \frac{N_1 \times N_2}{M_2} .$$

(4.2)

Question 4.5

(a) If 48 animals were originally marked and 100 captured on a second occasion, of which 15 were marked, what is the *estimated* total population size?

(b) This technique is based on several important assumptions. One of these has already been described (point 2 above) whilst a second is mentioned elsewhere. What is that second assumption?

Remember that this method can only provide an *estimate* of the size of populations; however, it has been used successfully on a wide variety of animal species, including insects, snails and small mammals.

4.2.5 Using the mean and variance of population size

In Activity 4.1, several ways of plotting the data on butterfly population size from Table 4.1 were discussed. Plotting population size against time provided a visual summary of the fluctuations in population. This section looks briefly at the benefits of a *quantitative* summary of those fluctuations, which complements the graphical approach.

Any set of numerical data, whether it be numbers of animals, sizes of plants, or the number of doors in houses, can be summarized in two ways. The first way is to calculate a mean, or average, which summarizes quantitatively a set of numbers by giving an average value for that set of numbers.

Question 4.6
Calculate the mean population size over the years 1978–87 for the chalkhill blue and marbled white butterflies, using the data in Table 4.1 (Section 4.2.2). Indicate the position of the means on your graphs of these population fluctuations over time (Activity 4.1).

The second method of summarizing numerical data is to quantify the spread of numbers around the mean, i.e. the variation around the mean. This is achieved by calculating the variance or standard deviation. Variance is calculated by finding the difference between each data value and the mean, squaring those differences, and adding them up. This so-called sum of squares is then divided by the number of values (sometimes subtracting one) to produce a value for the variance. If the square root of the variance is taken, then this gives the standard deviation. Applying these statistical techniques to the data set in Table 4.1 produces values for the marbled white of variance 139 000 and standard deviation 373. The corresponding values for the chalkhill blue are 1 210 000 and standard deviation 1 100. (If you have mathematical leanings and/or access to a suitable calculator, you could check these values for yourself!)

▷ Do the values of standard deviation for the chalkhill blue and marbled white agree with the visual presentation of the fluctuations in your graphs of population size against time from Figure 4.9 (answer to Activity 4.1)?

▶ Not obviously! The standard deviation for the chalkhill blue (1 100) is about three times that of the marbled white (373). The graphs in Figure 4.9 do not show clearly that the variation in the size of the chalkhill blue population is greater than that of the marbled white.

A major reason for this discrepancy is that the mean of the chalkhill blue is about six times larger than that of the marbled white, so we would expect a larger standard deviation. So, although standard deviation can be a very revealing measure of the spread of a succession of values around the mean value, as in these butterfly data, it may not be sufficient in itself. In making comparisons between species, one often needs to take account of the mean, standard deviation, and the general trends in the data.

4.3 The orang-utan in Borneo

Up to now, we have talked about the assessment of species and populations in rather theoretical terms, one step removed from the practical problems that conservationists face 'in the field'. At this point it would be useful to step back into the real world and consider a practical example of modern conservation. We do so by discussing a scientific paper on the orang-utan in one area of Borneo. The paper—*The orang-utan in Sabah*—is reproduced in its entirety as Extract 4.1.

Activity 4.2   *You should spend up to 1 hour on this activity.*

Begin by skim-reading Extract 4.1 in order to familiarize yourself with its structure, the main issues that are addressed, and the conclusions reached. Note the initial summary in the first paragraph; nowadays, in an area like conservation, such a great wealth of material is published that the summary may well be the only part of a paper that is widely read, so it needs to be both concise and informative.

Next, read the paper through carefully and try to pick out what you feel are the most significant points. Make notes if it helps to absorb the details. Try not to refer to the paper or to your notes (except when told to) as you tackle questions (a)–(h), which are designed to test your recollection and understanding of what you have read.

(a) Why was the area of Sabah chosen for study?

(b) Identify aspects of the animal's behaviour that (i) hinder, and (ii) aid location of the orang-utan.

(c) Which sampling technique was employed, and which alternative technique mentioned earlier in this chapter might be applicable?

(d) What do you understand by the phrase 'too few data were collected to make a statistical assessment of the accuracy of the population densities obtained'?

(e) The author suggests there are at least 4 000 orang-utan in the primary forest area in eastern Sabah. How do you think this value was obtained?

(f) Examine Table 1 in the extract carefully. What firm conclusions about the effects of logging on orang-utan populations can be drawn?

(g) What is the principal recommendation from the paper to ensure the future survival of the orang-utan?

(h) Identify one area of current uncertainty where future research will be most likely to help produce an effective conservation policy.

Extract 4.1   From *Oryx*, **20**, 1 January 1986, pp. 40–45.

The orang-utan in Sabah

Glyn Davies

A survey of orang-utans in Sabah, Borneo, which was carried out by the author and John Payne, resulted in an encouraging picture. In the primary forest of eastern Sabah alone, there are at least 4 000 orang-utans, but habitat destruction is fragmenting the population. Hunting is also common, especially in the central and western areas where orang-utans are already scarce. Some orang-utans are protected in conservation areas, but the future of the species outside these places depends on logging being carried out in a more conservation-oriented way. Among other things, we need to discover the size of primary-forest patches that need to be left in logged forest to support a viable population of orang-utans, which will be able to recolonize the logged forest as it regenerates.

The orang-utan *Pongo pygmaeus* is Asia's great ape and it occurs on only two islands in South-East Asia. On Sumatra it is restricted to upland forests in the northern part of the island, but the species is more widespread in Borneo (Rijksen, 1978). One area in Borneo where the orang-utan has attracted much attention is Sabah, the State occupying the northern 76 115 sq.km of the island. During the 1960s, surveys and ecological studies revealed dense populations of orang-utans in some regions (Davenport, 1967; MacKinnon, 1971; Horr, 1972), and some areas were recommended for conservation of the species. These recommendations came to little, however, and there have been drastic changes in land use over the last 20 years. As a result, in 1979 the Wildlife Section of the Sabah Forest Department initiated a faunal survey of the State to investigate the distribution and abundance of mammal populations, paying particular attention to large, endangered species such as the orang-utan. The survey was coordinated by two investigators who were funded by the World Wildlife Fund Malaysia (Payne and Davies, 1982).

Orang-utans are shy animals and are difficult to see in the dense vegetation of the rain forest, despite their large size and red pelage. They tend not to live in large family groups, but occur singly or in small parties of two to five animals. There are several features of the animals' biology, however, that aid their location. Adult male orang-utans give loud roaring calls, and animals of all ages, excluding the smallest infants, give squeals and 'kiss-squeaks' when alarmed. They also make loud rustling sounds in branches as they travel between tree crowns. Occasionally, the larger animals travel along the ground and leave footprints. Furthermore, all independent animals build a nest-platform to sleep in each night, which, if it is recently built, indicates the presence of orang-utans in an area.

During the two-and-a-half year project, all sightings of orang-utans, their signs and reliable reports of their presence were recorded. In addition, detailed information was collected on orang-utan population densities at 20 sites during surveys, which lasted between 6 and 9 days. At each site an 80-m wide transect of forest was surveyed. This transect width represented the distance either side of a trail over which primates could be reliably detected by an observer walking slowly through the forest. Too few data were collected to make a statistical assessment of the accuracy of the population density estimates obtained using this method, but the results from three survey sites tallied closely with those obtained during long-term studies of orang-utans in the same areas.

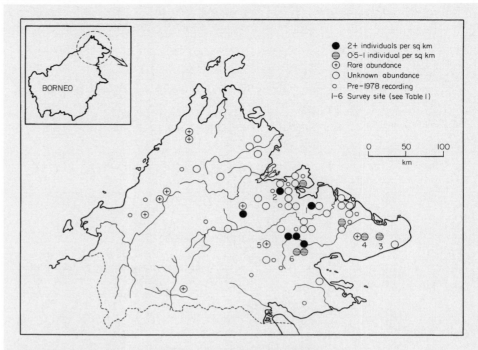

Figure 1   Distribution and abundance of orang-utans in Sabah.

The orang-utan population

A map of the distribution of orang-utans within Sabah (Figure 1) is encouraging, in that it shows that the species is still widely distributed. Few surveys were made to the poorly accessible south/central part of Sabah and so records from this region are incomplete, but there is no reason to expect orang-utans to be absent, although they may be scarce. The densest populations were found in primary forests of the eastern lowlands (less than 150 m above sea level) where there were up to two orang-utans per sq. km. At other sites in the eastern region (less than 450 m above sea level) population densities ranged from 0.5 to 1 individual per sq. km. Orang-utan populations in Sabah become sparser with increasing altitude (Figure 2), and they were so scarce

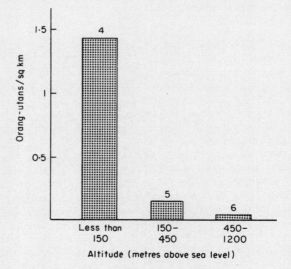

Figure 2   Average population densities of orang-utans at different altitudes in Sabah. Numbers refer to the number of sites that were surveyed from each altitudinal zone.

in the highlands of western Sabah that it was impossible to estimate the numbers accurately. It is not clear to what extent this scarcity results from a decrease in the quality of forest for orang-utans as altitude increases, or how much hunting, which is common in western areas, has a negative effect.

Applying the above estimates of population density to primary forest areas in eastern Sabah (about 5 000 sq. km), it is calculated that there are at least 4 000 orang-utans in this area. There are some more orang-utans in the central region of the State, which was less thoroughly surveyed, but very few occur in the western areas. Overall, therefore, there is a substantial population of orang-utans in Sabah, which provides ample scope for conservation of the species.

Threats to the species

Although the large number of orang-utans found in Sabah is encouraging, the population is decreasing in size and is being fragmented. The main pressures on the population are hunting, habitat degradation through commercial selective felling, and loss of forest to agricultural schemes.

Hunting

In western and south-western Sabah, local people hunt orang-utans for food. This is a mountainous area where orang-utans are scarce, and there are many places where the species has been eliminated by hunting practices. A similar situation has been described for part of neighbouring Sarawak (Medway, 1970). Recently, with the introduction of shotguns, the intensity of hunting has increased all over the State. In the east, timber-camp employees and town-dwellers occasionally shoot orang-utans for 'sport'. Law enforcement by the Forest Department has controlled hunting in these areas, but little can be done in the more remote central and western regions.

Timber extraction

Over 50 per cent of Sabah has been selectively logged, which, in conjunction with agricultural schemes, leaves only one-third of the State covered by primary forest, mainly in south/central areas. The effects of timber extraction on orang-utans in Sabah were assessed during six surveys in the eastern part of the State. Two surveys were made in Virgin Jungle Reserves, which are isolated primary forest areas of less than 500 ha surrounded by logged forest. Four surveys were made in two pairs in two regions: one survey from each pair was done in logged forest 15–20 years after timber had been extracted, and the other in nearby primary forest (see Table 1).

One immediate effect of timber extraction is that a small number of orang-utans are killed during felling. Most, however, emigrate to areas of undisturbed forest, even if this results in crowding. The population densities recorded in the two Virgin Jungle Reserves were twice as high as expected for the region, especially since surveys in the same areas revealed low orang-utan population densities in the 1960s (Harrisson, 1963).

In cases where orang-utans migrate to large tracts of primary forest, the resident populations tend to become overcrowded by this influx from logged forests. This, in turn, may result in a decline in birth rate (MacKinnon, 1972). Thus, while the migration of orang-utans may reduce immediate fatalities, stable populations are unlikely to be bolstered in the long-term by immigration.

Once timber extraction has ceased, many areas of logged forest in Sabah are left to regenerate.

Table 1 The influence of timber extraction on orang-utan populations in Sabah (surveys made in 1980/81).

Survey site	Altitude/ m	Habitat	Population density/ individuals per sq. km
1. Gomantong	30	Virgin Jungle Reserve	3.9
2. Lungmanis	40	Virgin Jungle Reserve	4.1
3. Bakapit	150	Logged in 1962 (8 per ha*)	0
4. Tabin	170	Primary forest	?
5. Malubuk	220	Logged in 1965 (10 per ha*)	?
6. Kawag	220	Primary forest	1.0

?, present but rare; *, number of trees removed.

Surveys of logged forest in an area where orang-utans were probably abundant prior to logging (for example, Malubuk) revealed that some orang-utans did occur in the logged forest, although at much lower densities than in primary forests of the same region. In areas where orang-utans were probably only moderately common prior to logging (for example, Bakapit) none were recorded in logged forest. Overall, therefore, the species is particularly vulnerable to changes in its habitat and is largely dependent on primary forests for its survival.

It is encouraging that some orang-utans occur in a few logged forests, but it is unclear whether these animals have always been in the areas or have recolonized them recently. It is also not known whether they live wholly in the logged forests or are merely passing through between patches of primary forest. More information is needed on these ecological questions, and on the breeding success of animals living in logged forests, before the usefulness of logged forests for orang-utan conservation can be fully assessed.

Agriculture

The other major form of habitat alteration is agricultural development of an area. In Sabah, traditional shifting cultivators clear small areas of forest (less than 10 ha), burn the trees and plant hill rice and fruit trees for about three years before moving on. This results in a mosaic of habitats, to which orang-utans can adapt as long as the hunting pressure, which often accompanies shifting cultivation, is not too great. Unfortunately, orang-utans feed from fruit trees that are near forest edges on occasions and are consequently shot as pests.

As the scale of forest clearance and burning increases, so the ability of orang-utans to use the area decreases. As a result, few orang-utans have been recorded in western areas of Sabah, where settled agriculturalists clear and burn large areas of hill forest for rice. Similarly, modern agricultural development, for which over 30 per cent of Sabah is suitable, involves the clear felling and burning of many hundreds of hectares. The initial burning of vegetation eliminates all wildlife, and orang-utans do not feed to any great extent on the cash crops that are subsequently planted. Unfortunately, the best agricultural land in Sabah is found in the eastern lowlands, where the densest populations of orang-utans have been found and where some orang-utans survive in logged forests.

Conservation

The deleterious effects of hunting, timber extraction and agricultural development mean that the only way to preserve orang-utans is by setting aside areas of primary forest where there is little hunting. Only small populations of orang-utans, however, are represented in the present conservation areas in Sabah (Figure 3).

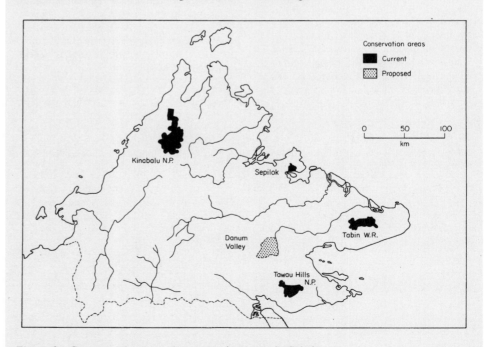

Figure 3 Current and proposed conservation areas in Sabah.

At Sepilok, an Orang-Utan Centre was established in 1964 with the aim of reintroducing captive orang-utans into the wild (de Silva, 1970). Although there are many problems in rehabilitating orang-utans (Aveling and Mitchell, 1982), the Centre has an important function as a place to which confiscated animals may be taken. In addition, the Wildlife Education Centre there is important in informing local people of Sabah's wildlife and has more than 25 000 visitors each year. In terms of preserving a population of orang-utans in the long-term, however, Sepilok—only 40 sq. km in area—is probably too small. The two inland national parks of Sabah, Kinabalu and Tawau Hills, also have very few orang-utans; indeed, the latter seems to have none at all.

The recently gazetted Tabin Wildlife Reserve (1 205 sq. km), therefore, is the only area where a population of orang-utans has legal protection. There are about 100 sq. km of primary forest in this Reserve, where moderate densities of orang-utans have been recorded (less than one animal per sq. km). This situation would be greatly improved if legal protection were extended to preserve the Danum Valley area (438 sq. km) in eastern Sabah. This area has long been recommended for wildlife conservation since it is expected to have a large population of orang-utans, it probably harbours the Sumatran rhinoceros, and it is unsuitable for agriculture. The area is within the Ulu Segama Forest Reserve and is part of the Sabah Foundation's timber concession area. Current policies of the Forest Department and the Sabah Foundation have excluded the Danum Valley from immediate plans for timber exploitation, and if these policies can be realized in terms of long-term legal protection, the preservation of Sabah's orang-utans should be assured.

In the future, large areas of Borneo that are unsuitable for agriculture will be covered by logged forest. It has been noted that some primates can survive selective logging of dipterocarp forests in South-East Asia, and that ungulates may prefer logged areas to primary forests (Johns, 1983), but this does not apply to orang-utans and other forest-dependent animals. It may be possible, however, to combine wildlife conservation with timber extraction if small areas of primary forest are left in logged areas. Research is needed to investigate the minimum size of primary forest areas that can support populations of animals until they can recolonize the surrounding logged areas, since this may take between 20 and 40 years. It is also necessary to examine how many primary forest areas would be needed in logged regions and at what intervals timber could be extracted from around them to ensure that no species were lost.

This information should make it possible to manage forests so that both animals that are tolerant and those that are intolerant of habitat alteration will be preserved in multiple-use forests containing a diversity of vegetation types. This will make maximum use of large tracts of logged forest for wildlife conservation. However, such a wildlife management policy can only be effective if hunting and agricultural practices in logged forests are restricted, and the temptation to cut the easily accessible primary forest patches resisted. With such imponderables, it is still imperative to set aside and maintain large areas of primary forest in order to preserve animals and plants that cannot tolerate habitat disruption. The value of logged forests that contain small primary forest reserves, however, should not be overlooked. This habitat may preserve even primary-forest dependent species, as has been shown during these surveys of orang-utans in Sabah.

Acknowledgments

The Faunal Survey of Sabah project was supported by Mr P. M. Andau (Assistant Chief Wildlife Warden), and personnel of the Wildlife Section, Sabah Forest Department, participated in all surveys. Mr L. Ali (Director of Sabah National Parks) encouraged surveys in national parks, and staff from this office joined these surveys. World Wildlife Fund Malaysia sponsored the two survey co-ordinators through a donation from Tractors Malaysia Berhad. Constructive criticism of drafts of this paper was given by J. B. Payne, A. D. Johns, E. B. M. Barrett, E. L. Bennett, G. L. de Silva, C. W. Marsh and S. M. O'Connor.

References

Aveling, R. J. and Mitchell, A. (1982) Is rehabilitating orang-utans worthwhile? *Oryx*, **XVI**, pp. 263–271.

Davenport, R. K. (1967) The orangutan in Sabah, *Folia primatol*, **5**, pp. 247–263.

Harrisson, B. (1963) *Report of censuses in sample habitat areas of North Borneo*, unpublished World Wildlife Fund report.

Horr, D. A. (1972) The Borneo orangutan, *Borneo Research Bulletin*, **4**, pp. 46–50.

Johns, A. D. (1983) Tropical forest primates and logging—can they co-exist? *Oryx*, **XVII**, pp. 114–118.

MacKinnon, J. R. (1971) The orangutan in Sabah today, *Oryx*, **XI**, pp. 141–191.

MacKinnon, J. R. (1972) *The behaviour and ecology of the orangutan (Pongo pygmaeus), with relation to other apes*, D. Phil. Thesis, University of Oxford.

Medway, Lord (1970) *The Mammals of Borneo*, Malaysian Branch of the Royal Asiatic Society.

Payne, J. B. and Davies, A. G. (1982) *A Faunal Survey of Sabah*, World Wildlife Fund Malaysia.

Rijksen, H. D. (1978) *A Field Study of Sumatran Orangutans* (Pongo pygmaeus abelli): *Ecology, Behaviour and Conservation*, Wageningen, Netherlands.

Silva, G. S. de (1970) Training orangutans for the wild, *Oryx*, **X**, pp. 389–393.

4.4 Using data on population size

Earlier in this chapter, we noted the difficulty of identifying which species needed conserving. We are now in a position to consider how data on population size might be used to help identify populations or species which require protection or management.

To begin with, it is important to define the **probability of extinction** for a population. Probability quantifies the chance of an event occurring. A coin tossed in the air has a probability of 1/2 (1 in 2, or 50%) of landing heads up and 1/2 of landing tails up. The probability of a rolled die landing with a 3 uppermost is 1/6. We can define probabilities of extinction for populations in the same way. A population might have a 1 in 10 chance of becoming extinct in any one year, so its probability of extinction is 1/10 (10%). A species with populations that have a high probability of extinction is an obvious candidate for conservation.

Why is it necessary to define a *probability* of extinction? The simple answer is that the natural fluctuations in population size over time, as seen for the chalkhill blue and marbled white butterflies (Figure 4.9, answer to Activity 4.1), may be quite large and in any year there is the possibility that the fluctuation will be sufficiently large to cause the population to become extinct. An estimate of the probability of extinction allows us to quantify that possibility. (Remember that these fluctuations can result in the population size increasing as well as decreasing.)

The probability of an 'extinction event' occurring in any one year can be related to the mean population size and its variance over time.

▷ Which of two populations with equal mean size but different variances will have the higher probability of extinction in any one year?

▶ The population size with the higher variance will have a higher probability of extinction because its fluctuations are larger, giving rise to very low population sizes from time to time, and therefore a greater risk of extinction.

▷ Which two populations with equal variances, but different mean values, will have the higher probability of extinction?

▶ The population with the lower mean value, because the same fluctuations will result in lower population values.

This shows that there is a relationship between mean, variance and probability of extinction, which will be examined more fully in Section 4.4.1 when a method of estimating the probability of population extinction will be developed. However, before this it is important to distinguish between three types of extinction.

1   One type of extinction, which was referred to previously, depends only on fluctuations in the population size (it can be assumed that there is no change in the mean population size, Figure 4.4a), perhaps caused by external chance events such as weather patterns—therefore it is appropriate to use probabilities to quantify this type of extinction.

2   The second type of extinction occurs because the mean population size reduces over time, such that the population is driven towards extinction (Figure 4.4b). This may be caused by a variety of factors, such as habitat loss.

3   The final type of extinction combines the first two types, i.e. a population with a declining mean size, which also fluctuates about the mean (Figure 4.4c).

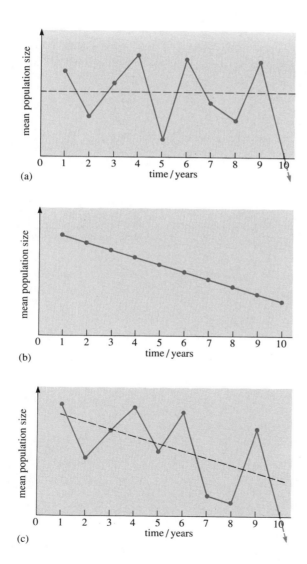

Figure 4.4   Types of population extinction. (a) Extinction due to fluctuations around a constant mean population size (shown by the dashed line). (b) Extinction due to a declining mean population size. (c) Extinction due to fluctuations around a declining mean population size (shown by the dashed line).

We will now use a simple mathematical model of population dynamics to estimate the probability of extinction. Some relevant principles of population dynamics and mathematical models are discussed in Box 4.1.

4.1

Box 4.1   Population dynamics and mathematical models

The term **population dynamics** means changes in the size of a population over time, e.g. the fluctuations in observed numbers of the chalkhill blue and marbled white butterflies over time (Table 4.1). Population dynamics may involve an increase, a decrease or no change in population size. In **mathematical models** the aim is to summarize, describe or mimic the behaviour of a system using mathematical equations. The 'system' might be a biological population or the cars on a motorway or the chemical reactants in a test-tube. A typical mathematical model of population dynamics includes the mean number of offspring produced per year (or other time interval) from animals or plants of particular ages, known as *age-specific* **fecundity**, and the mean fraction of individuals dying at each age, *age-specific* **mortality**. For some species it is more useful to employ either *size*-specific or *stage*-specific fecundities and mortalities. Thus, plants of a particular *size* will tend to produce, on average, a certain number of offspring (seed) in one year, and have a certain chance of dying. Similarly, one *stage* in the life cycle of an animal or plant, such as the larval stage of a fly, can be assigned a specific mortality value.

If *constant* values of fecundity and mortality are assumed, the population will either increase with time, decline towards extinction, or not change (Figure 4.5). However, there are problems when applying population dynamics to real populations based on the assumptions of constant mortality and fecundity. First, these values are never constant, but fluctuate with external climatic factors such as rainfall and temperature. Second, fecundity and mortality values are often dependent on the number of individuals present. So, if a population is very large, the number of offspring produced per individual may be reduced.

▷   Can you think of a mechanism which might produce this effect of reduced fecundity with increased population size?

▶   If the population is large, food may be scarce: this will result in smaller females which in turn could reduce the number of offspring produced.

Population size is most conveniently represented as numbers (i.e. *x* individuals) per unit area or volume. This is referred to as the **population density** (see examples of the use of this term in Extract 4.1). If mortality and fecundity are *un*related to density, i.e. population size, they are termed **density *independent***. If they are affected by density they are referred to as **density-dependent**. ■

Figure 4.5   Three types of population dynamics produced by constant values of age-specific mortality and fecundity. (a) Increasing population size with time, (b) no change in population size, and (c) declining population size with time. Condition (b), no change, is produced by very precise population conditions in which deaths are exactly balanced by births.

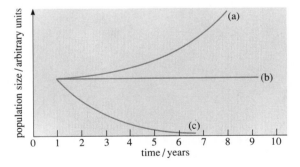

4.4.1   A mathematical model for predicting probabilities of extinction

Let us start by assuming that a population has a certain initial size at time 1. The individuals in this population have constant mean values of fecundity and *survival* at different ages. (Survival is used rather than death—mortality—because it makes the calculations easier.) Let us assume that under constant conditions this population will have one of the three types of dynamics described in Figure 4.5 by choosing a model

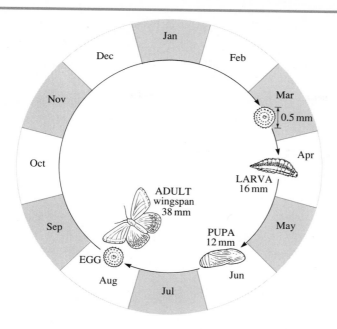

Figure 4.6 Life cycle of the chalkhill blue butterfly (*Lysandra coridon*). The butterfly spends the winter as an egg, and emerges as a larva in April. The larvae (caterpillars) feed predominantly on horseshoe vetch (*Hippocrepis comosa*) during April, May and June, and pupate during June and July, to emerge as adults at the end of July or August. When adult, the butterfly then lays eggs and dies.

species which breeds only once a year and then dies after reproduction. This could be an insect species such as a butterfly or moth; in fact, the chalkhill blue butterfly is a good example. Its life cycle is shown in Figure 4.6—many other species follow similar life cycles.

There may be death at any stage in the life cycle, i.e. not all of the eggs will survive to become larvae, nor all of the larvae to become pupae, etc. If we assume that at the end of the butterfly year (August) we have 100 eggs and that a constant fraction (92%) survive through the winter to emerge as larvae in the following April, then:

100 eggs give 92 larvae.

From the 92 larvae feeding during April, May and early June, assume that 55% (again a constant each year) survive until pupation:

92 larvae × 0.55 give 50.6 pupae. (It is possible to have 0.6 of a pupa for calculation purposes!)

Finally, assume 75% of the pupae survive to emerge as adults at the end of July:

50.6 pupae × 0.75 give 37.95 adults.

Therefore, of the original 100 eggs at the end of the previous year (August) only 37.95 have become adults by the end of the next year. At each point in the life cycle a survival value, as required for the model, is fixed. All the survival values are then combined to give an *overall survival value* of 0.379 5 from egg to adult:

100 eggs × 0.92 (egg survival) × 0.55 (larval survival) × 0.75 (pupal survival)

= 100 × 0.379 5

= 37.95 adults.

▷ What else do we need to know in order to calculate the number of eggs produced by the 37.95 adults?

▶ We require the mean fecundity *per adult*. This will be the mean number of fertilized eggs produced *per female* divided by two (assuming a sex ratio of 1:1).

Let the mean number of fertilized eggs per female be 40. Therefore each adult 'produces' an average of 20 eggs. We can now complete the simple population model:

100 eggs in August of year *t* produce 37.95 adults by late July of year *t* + 1, which then produce 37.95 × 20 = 759 eggs.

The **multiplication rate** of a population is defined as the number of eggs produced in year *t* + 1 for every egg in year *t*.

▷ What is the multiplication rate of our model population?

▶ It is the number of eggs in year *t* + 1, i.e. 759, divided by the number of eggs in year *t* (i.e. 100), which equals 759/100 = 7.59. (Note that the multiplication rate is measured between equivalent life cycle stages, e.g. from egg to egg or adult to adult.)

In fact, if the survival and fecundity values remain constant from year to year, the population will increase by a multiple of 7.59 *every* year.

Question 4.7 If a population starts at 100 eggs in year 1 (*t*), and has increased to 250 by year 2 (*t* + 1), what is the multiplication rate? If this rate is constant, what is the size of the population in years 3 and 4?

Therefore we have reached the important conclusion that a population composed of individuals with constant fecundity and survival values will have a constant *rate* of increase (or decrease), as shown in Figure 4.5. It is also possible that the (constant) fecundity value could exactly balance the (constant) survival value, resulting in a steady state with no increase or decrease (Figure 4.5b). These ideas are explored in Activity 4.3.

Activity 4.3 *You should spend up to 30 minutes on this activity.*

Assume that there are three different butterfly populations, all of which begin with 10 eggs. The multiplication rates of these three populations are 2, 1 and 0.5, respectively.

(a) Plot the change in population size from year 1 to year 4 for each population.

(b) How would you describe the change in population size of each of these three populations?

(c) What is the multiplication rate required for populations *not* to become extinct?

(d) Is the suggestion here of a population increasing at a multiplication rate of 2 realistic?

(e) Finally, try replotting the data using a logarithmic scale for the population sizes, i.e. calculate the $\log_{10}$ (population size) value and plot this against time. What advantage does the logarithmic scale have over the graphs plotted in (a)?

We can now consider a more realistic model, in which the multiplication rate is *not* constant but fluctuates. Let us also assume that the factors causing fluctuations are external to the individuals (e.g. weather), and do not necessarily have the same effect each year. In fact we are going to assume that they are random in their operation, i.e. there are good and bad years that are unpredictable in their occurrence over time.

The unpredictable environmental factors could affect the multiplication rate of the population in a variety of ways. For example, high rainfall might reduce the survival rate of eggs whilst unusually low temperatures might reduce the survival of pupae.

Under constant conditions the population will become extinct only if its multiplication rate is less than 1 (as in Figure 4.5c and Activity 4.3c). In order to explore the effect of fluctuations on extinction let us for simplicity take a population with a multiplication rate of exactly 1. As you know from Activity 4.3, under constant conditions such a population will neither become extinct nor will it increase in size. However, we now take into account that there are good and bad years, simulated by throwing a die. The numbers 1–6 represent very bad (1) through to very good (6) years:

Throwing a 1, 2 or 3 *reduces* the multiplication rate to:

> one-tenth (throwing a 1),
>
> one-half (throwing a 2), or
>
> three-quarters (throwing a 3) of its original value.

Throwing a 4, 5 or 6 *increases* the multiplication rate to:

> four-thirds (throwing a 4),
>
> two times (throwing a 5), or
>
> ten times (throwing a 6) its original value.

Over a long period of time, and assuming that the die is unbiased, the population would be expected to fluctuate around its initial size because the increases and decreases produced by throws of the die cancel out, for example, throwing a 1 followed by a 6 produces $1/10 \times 10 = 1$ (similarly, $1/2 \times 2 = 1$, $4/3 \times 3/4 = 1$). There will, however, be the possibility of *several bad years in a row* that could result in the population becoming extinct if it starts from a low initial size.

If we use initial population sizes of 1 and 5 and a multiplication rate of 1, it is possible to find out how rapidly each model population would become extinct by throwing a die to simulate the change in the multiplication rate. This simulation was stopped after 20 throws of the die if the population had not become extinct and repeated five times for each initial population size. An arbitrary extinction value of greater than zero was set (in this case 0.5) because the population could never reach zero given the assumptions made. For example, if there are five very bad years in a row, starting from an initial population size of 1 would give $1 \times 1/10 \times 1/10 \times 1/10 \times 1/10 \times 1/10$, which equals $(1/10)^5$, or 0.00001, or 1×10^{-5}. (Look at Figure 4.10 again in the answer to Activity 4.3 if you do not understand why the population, although declining, does not reach zero.) So, given the assumptions of the model, the population moves towards zero but never reaches it. However, we can assume that if the population size falls *below 0.5* it will become extinct.

The following example should clarify the procedure. Let us start with a population size of 5:

Population size at time 1 = 5.

The die is thrown, which we assume lands on 3. This means that the multiplication rate is reduced to 3/4 of its initial value of 1, i.e. 3/4.

So the population size at time 2 is 5×1 (multiplication rate) $\times 3/4 = 3.75$.

The die is thrown again, and lands on 1, which means that the multiplication rate is reduced to 1/10. The population size at time 3 is $3.75 \times 0.1 = 0.375$.

The population has now fallen below the arbitrary extinction level of 0.5 and is therefore 'extinct'. If the population is still in existence after 20 throws, then its final size is recorded. The results of the modelling exercise are displayed in Figure 4.7.

We have now reached an important point in our modelling, in that we can estimate the probability of extinction, given an initial population size.

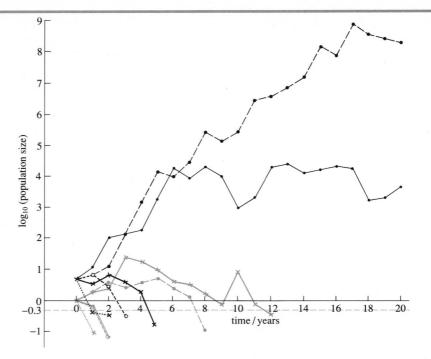

Figure 4.7 The results of the modelling exercise, simulating the change in population size over time from two initial population values: 1 (green, starting at $\log_{10}(1) = 0$) and 5 (black, starting at $\log_{10}(5) = 0.7$). The population size is given as $\log_{10}$ (population size). Notice that in all five runs of the model from an initial size of 1 the population becomes 'extinct', i.e. below 0.5 (its $\log_{10}$ equivalent is −0.3) within 20 years. The dashed line at −0.3 is the extinction line.

▷ With an initial population size of 1 (a $\log_{10}$ (population size) of 0), what was the probability of extinction within the 20-year time period?

▶ All five populations became extinct, so the probability of extinction was 5/5 = 1.0.

▷ With an initial population size of 5, what was the probability of extinction within 20 years?

▶ Three out of five populations became extinct, so the probability of extinction was 3/5 = 0.6.

Therefore these results suggest that a larger initial population size has a lower probability of extinction—an obvious result, with hindsight! It is also possible to calculate the average time for a population of a given initial size to become extinct; in the case of an initial population size of 1 the average time for the population to become extinct was 5 years.

▷ How could this modelling exercise be improved without altering the rules of the model?

▶ There are several possibilities for improvement whilst retaining the basic design of the model. The number of trials (5) for each initial population size is very low and could be increased. One could also try other initial population sizes, e.g. 3 or 10.

Question 4.8 Would you expect the results of the modelling exercise to have been the same if you had done it yourself?

Finally, it is worth noting that one would be driven mad by throwing the die 100 or 200 times to achieve a reasonable number of trials! A short cut is to incorporate the rules of the model into a computer program and allow the computer to generate the throws of the die for us. We can also produce a program that will calculate the probability of extinction, the mean time for the population to become extinct, and then plot out the results.

The approach so far in this section has made a number of important simplifying assumptions concerning the characteristics of biological populations. In particular it made the assumption that population sizes may over time continually increase or decrease (until extinction). This is unlikely—real populations often seem to return to a mean size over time. Some populations appear to be consistently large whilst others seem to be consistently small. Populations that persist within certain levels over long periods of time are presumed to be regulated in some way—by definition they have not previously declined to extinction and, whilst they may occasionally reach very high densities, their numbers will then drop. An important discovery in ecology has been the mechanism underlying this regulation, referred to as density-dependent change in survival/mortality or fecundity (Box 4.1). For example, as the density of organisms increases so there may be an increase in the fraction of individuals dying per unit of time, i.e. mortality is no longer constant (for a particular age, size or stage) but is determined by the density of the organisms.

One result of density dependence is that the population can achieve a *stable equilibrium* (steady-state or no change) size over a range of mortality and fecundity values. The population will tend to return to this stable equilibrium over time. This is in contrast to a population in which the individuals have constant mortality and fecundity, i.e. an *unstable equilibrium*, where it stays at the same value (under constant conditions) only if the multiplication rate is *exactly* 1. If the multiplication rate increases or decreases slightly, the population will not return to that (unstable) equilibrium. Although a population with density dependence may not stay precisely at its (stable) equilibrium value because of environmental fluctuations, it always tends to return to it. We will consider the ideas of stability and equilibrium further in Chapter 6.

4.4.2 Population Viability Analysis (PVA)

The application of population dynamics (such as that explored in Section 4.4.1) to the conservation of rare species has come to be known as **population viability analysis (PVA)**. A fundamental aim of PVA is to estimate the probability of extinction and the **minimum viable population size (MVP)** for a particular species. The definition of MVP appears both straightforward and appealing—what number of individuals of a particular species are required to enable a population to persist? Below this number the population will decline to extinction; above this number the population will persist.

A leading conservation biologist has commented about MVP 'that there is no single value or "magic number" that has universal validity'. Now that you know something about the methods of estimating extinction you would probably agree! Indeed, the fact that we need to estimate a *probability* of extinction means that there *cannot* be one magic number! The results of the model in Section 4.4.1 showed that populations with a larger initial size had a lower probability of extinction. We could define MVP as the *initial* population size that reduces the probability of extinction (over a given period of time) to an 'acceptably' low level (e.g. a 1 in 100 chance of becoming extinct in 20 years). Defined in this way, MVP is determined by both the multiplication rate and the pattern of variation in, for example, climatic conditions (the pattern of rolls of a die).

Despite the problem of calculating MVP, it is interesting to consider the sizes of populations recommended as MVP. For example, work on the grizzly bear in North America has suggested an MVP of about 50, based on considerations of fluctuations in fecundity and mortality. Others have suggested values of 500 or more for other species, dependent upon the amount of variation in population size (as quantified by the variance and standard deviation). Many of these estimates have come from modelling work very similar to that covered in Section 4.4.1.

If an MVP value can be estimated, it could lead to a number of possible *intentional* abuses. Any harvestable animal or plant species above its MVP may be regarded as available for exploitation as a biological resource (Chapter 3). Similarly, habitat destruction could be justified *if* it was predicted that it still allowed a selection of species to remain above their MVP. *Un*intentional abuses and dilemmas arising from the concept of MVP and probability of extinction also abound. Conservation managers and organizations, presented with such numbers, have to make decisions. Should they divert their efforts to those species closest to the MVP, ignoring those that fall below it? Or should they let species near to or above the MVP get on with it and focus on the species below? Finally, it is worth remembering that, by its very nature, the *probability* of extinction is no guarantee for the practitioner (or the threatened population!): hypothetically, if one were faced with the last herd of white rhinoceros (*Ceratotherium simum*) in Africa, would it be helpful to know that, based on the results of a mathematical model, the population had a one in four chance of becoming extinct?

The final section of this chapter will attempt to illustrate how these ideas of probability of extinction are becoming increasingly popular for solving 'real world' conservation problems.

4.5 Constructing practical measures of species vulnerability

Section 4.4 briefly reviewed how, despite the apparent theoretical advantages, the use of probabilities of extinction and MVP present practical problems in field situations of knowing what to do when a population is close to its MVP or has a particular probability of extinction. However, for field studies, there is a more fundamental problem. At the moment the probability of extinction can only be obtained from a mathematical model; it is much more difficult to assess such a probability in the field.

▷ What would be needed to calculate a probability of population extinction in the field?

▶ One method would be to monitor a number of populations of different sizes over long periods of time (just like the model populations). The proportion that become extinct in that period would then be recorded. This means that detailed population studies (such as that for the early spider orchid, Section 4.2) are needed, for just a single species, repeated many times at different sites.

It is clear that some index of species vulnerability is required which takes into account the size and dynamics of populations. The most widely used index is that adopted by the International Union for Conservation of Nature and Natural Resources (IUCN). This index contains six categories, defined as follows:

Extinct   Species that are possibly extinct or near extinction.

Endangered   Species in danger of extinction, and whose survival is unlikely if the causal factors continue operating.

Vulnerable   Species believed likely to move into the 'endangered' category in the near future, if the causal factors continue operating.

Rare   Species with small world populations that are not at present 'endangered' or 'vulnerable' but that are at risk.

Indeterminate   Species known to be 'endangered', 'vulnerable' or 'rare' but about which there is not enough information to say which of these categories is appropriate.

Insufficiently known   Species that are suspected, but not definitely known, to belong to any of the above categories, because of lack of information.

The last two categories highlight the fact that basic data on population size and distribution are still lacking for many species. Although this is an unsatisfactory state of affairs, the 'indeterminate' and 'insufficiently known' categories, lumped together, constitute a well-defined category for many species. The 'extinct' category is generally quite straightforward, although you will recall the problem of knowing whether a species exists, let alone whether it is extinct (Chapter 2)! Much of what you have read in this chapter so far should lead you to question exactly how to allocate a species to the remaining three categories (endangered, vulnerable or rare).

The 'vulnerable' category appears to be an intermediate between 'rare' and 'endangered', so let us start by concentrating on the two extremes. We will consider an example with which you are familiar—the orang-utan (Section 4.3). In which category should it be placed? To be placed in the 'rare' category it should have a 'small world population'. Our studies of the probability of extinction (Figure 4.7) allow us to think of how 'small' (in theory) the population might be.

▷   What population size would be too small?

▶   One that reduced the population below a level at which the probability of extinction was defined as 'unacceptably' high (e.g. more than 1 in 100 every 20 years).

Of course there is still a highly subjective element in making such a judgement, and the issue of what is 'acceptable' or 'unacceptable' will be returned to later. What should be apparent at this stage is that theoretical considerations such as the probability of extinction provide a guide for thought and perhaps help us to see the problems more clearly, if not provide exact answers.

Returning to the orang-utan, it is certain that the populations are 'at risk'. Given enough time, and if the 'causal factors' continue to operate (e.g. hunting, logging and agricultural development), the survival of the species is unlikely. However, the phrase 'in danger of extinction', under the endangered category, seems too extreme. Perhaps 'vulnerable' is the best category. Clearly, the placing of the orang-utan in one of these categories is a highly subjective exercise. In fact, the orang-utan is placed within the 'endangered' category (1987).

The IUCN has produced a series of Red Data Books which gives the names of animal and plant species that fall into these various categories. Other related books, such as the *Collins Guide to Rare Mammals of the World* (J. A. Burton and B. Pearson, 1987), have used the IUCN information, combined with other sets of data, e.g. on population size, to produce modified IUCN categories. For comparison, Burton and Pearson's categories for mammals are given here, graded on a star system:

***** 'Endangered and likely to become extinct—or may already be extinct. Only survives in much reduced populations and is vulnerable to any new threats', e.g. blue whale (*Balaenoptera musculus*). There are 67 species in this category.

**** 'Endangered and likely to become extinct in the wild, but survives as a captive breeding population or under highly controlled conditions, such as zoos or isolated reserves, or as a reintroduction', e.g. orang-utan (*Pongo pygmaeus*). This category includes 19 species.

*** 'Some *sub*species (interpreted broadly to include discrete populations) endangered, and/or declining over most of range', e.g. gorilla (*Gorilla gorilla*, Figure 4.8), and the African elephant (*Loxodonta africana*, Figure 2.1). There are 395 species in this category.

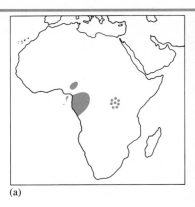

Figure 4.8 (a) The three subspecies of gorilla occur in two widely separated areas. The *western lowland gorilla* is found in rainforest in west Africa. About 1 000 km east are found the *eastern lowland gorilla* (b) in Zaire and the *mountain gorilla* on the borders of Zaire, Rwanda and Uganda.

(b)

** 'Occurs in small, isolated populations, is naturally rare and therefore vulnerable to any new threats. Or only known from a few observations. Species could be stable, but many, particularly those occurring in parts of the tropics where forest is being destroyed, could be highly endangered', e.g. tropical bats.

* 'Species considered by some authorities to be of conservation concern, but which are probably not threatened with imminent extinction', e.g. the Eurasian badger (*Meles meles*), which is found in Britain.

Question 4.9 What advantages can you see in this '5-star' system over the IUCN categories of extinct, endangered, vulnerable, rare, indeterminate, and insufficiently known?

More recently there have been attempts to use theories of population dynamics more explicitly within IUCN categories. Indeed, in the latest proposals, outlined in an paper by G. M. Mace and R. Lande in the scientific journal *Conservation Biology*, the categories are defined with respect to probability of population extinction. The abstract from that paper, along with definitions of the three categories of threat, are given in Extract 4.2 which you should read now.

Extract 4.2 From G. M. Mace and R. Lande, *Conservation Biology* (1991) **5**, pp. 148–157.

IUCN categories of threat (Endangered, Vulnerable, Rare, Indeterminate, and others) are widely used in 'Red lists' of endangered species and have become an important tool in conservation action at international, national, regional, and thematic levels. The existing definitions are largely subjective, and as a result, categorizations made by different authorities differ and may not accurately reflect actual extinction risks. We present proposals to redefine categories in terms of the probability of extinction within a specific time period, based on the theory of extinction times for single populations and on meaningful time scales for conservation action. Three categories are proposed (CRITICAL, ENDANGERED, VULNERABLE) with decreasing levels of threat over increasing time scales for species estimated to have at least a 10% probability of extinction within

100 years. The process of assigning species to categories may need to vary among different taxonomic groups, but we present some simple qualitative criteria based on population biology theory, which we suggest are appropriate at least for most large vertebrates. The process of assessing threat is clearly distinguished from that of setting priorities for conservation action, and only the former is discussed here.

We propose the recognition of three categories of threat (plus EXTINCT), defined as follows:

CRITICAL   50% probability of extinction within 5 years or 2 generations, whichever is longer.

ENDANGERED   20% probability of extinction within 20 years or 10 generations, whichever is longer.

VULNERABLE   10% probability of extinction within 100 years.

In employing these criteria, Mace and Lande are emphasizing the need for collection of appropriate and sufficient population data, by methods such as those described in the present chapter, along with a more detailed knowledge of habitat requirements of the species. Furthermore, including values such as probability of extinction show the use of theoretical details and mathematical models of the type employed in Section 4.4.

Summary of Chapter 4

1   The steps in sampling a population as a means of assessing population size include choosing a site (perhaps using presence/absence and distribution data), and then sampling directly or indirectly, often using traps for small mobile animals.

2   Population size can be summarized quantitatively using the mean and standard deviation (the variation around the mean).

3   Mathematical models provide a description of how population dynamics can determine the probability of population extinction.

4   Minimum viable population size can be defined with respect to the probability of extinction; for example, a minimum viable population is one that reduces the probability of extinction (over a given time) to an acceptably low level. These theoretical ideas are increasingly becoming part of the IUCN thinking on classifying endangered species.

Activity 4.4   *You should spend up to 20 minutes on this activity.*

(a) Imagine that you are asked to determine the feasibility of estimating the size of the orang-utan population in Sabah using a mark–release–recapture technique. Outline the methods you would use (a summary in note form would be suitable) and any problems you might encounter.

(b) Now consider that you are asked to construct a mathematical model to predict the change in size of the orang-utan population over time. Without worrying about the details of constructing the model, what pieces of field data would you require to produce such a model? (Hint: look back at the elements we included in the butterfly model in Section 4.4.1.)

---

5 Management of habitats and species

The link between declining numbers of species and habitat loss or degradation has been examined throughout Chapters 2–4. Faced with a species whose numbers are decreasing, the cause of decline needs first to be identified. Armed with that knowledge, this rate of decline then needs to be reversed or reduced. For some species it may be simply enough to stop the current threat, such as deforestation, and allow the habitat, and therefore the particular species, to recover. For other species and habitats, a more active approach is required. Specifically, the species and/or its habitat need to be *managed* in order to restore population size to 'acceptable' levels (as discussed in Section 4.5). Most frequently it is management of the *habitat* rather than management of the species that is most appropriate. An advantage of managing the habitat is that one may help not only the targeted species but also other species resident in that habitat.

In this and the next chapter, several extracts from scientific papers will be used that will give a flavour of the way in which scientific information on conservation and ecology is communicated. Bear in mind that most scientific papers are written by specialist authors for the benefit of other specialists, so they are not always easily accessible for the interested layperson. Scientific papers usually follow a conventional structure with the following sections: Summary or Abstract, Introduction, Methods, Results, Discussion or Conclusion, and References; examples of these will be used in Chapters 5 and 6.

5.1 Habitat management and secondary succession

Habitat management is a daily routine for many people involved in conservation in Britain and elsewhere. What many of them are attempting to do is to keep ecological succession in check. You will recall from Chapter 2 that succession was described as the natural change in the composition of plant and animal species over time, from habitats dominated by grasses and other small plants, to woodland dominated by large trees. In fact there are two types of succession (Box 5.1), which arise under very different circumstances.

5.1

Box 5.1   Primary and secondary succession

A **primary succession** is one that begins on a substrate with no soil, an example being a newly formed volcanic island. The early stages of a primary succession are often characterized by very harsh conditions, such as large temperature fluctuations or low water availability. Under these circumstances only certain simple species such as lichens will survive and reproduce. One group of plants that do well in the early stages of a primary succession, once some form of soil is present, are nitrogen-fixing species. These species, such as some of those in the plant family Leguminosae (which includes peas and beans), have a mutualistic association (i.e. one in which both species benefit) with *Rhizobium* bacteria which live in root nodules. These bacteria can convert atmospheric nitrogen gas to a form that plants can use.

As the density and living mass of plants increase in the early stages of a primary succession so soils develop from accumulating organic matter and weathered rock particles, creating conditions suitable for new plant species. With these new plant species may come associated animal species, such as insects. In this way primary succession develops. In Britain, a range of examples of primary succession can be seen, such as on abandoned quarry sites like those on the magnesian limestone of County Durham (Plate 5.1).

Conservationists are normally concerned with **secondary succession**, which begins on soil cleared of its original vegetation. The methods of clearance include physical removal of vegetation (e.g. logging or ploughing) and fire, and thus influence the rate and course of succession.

It is possible in some areas to see examples of many steps along a sequence of secondary succession. In Figure 5.1, habitats (a), (b), (c) and (d) represent four stages in a secondary succession. Habitat (a) is mainly bare earth with few plants. The characteristic plant species are typically short-lived, such as annuals,

that can complete their life cycle from seed to flowering plant and seed set in 1 year. Habitat (b) is grassland characterized by a mixture of perennial grasses and other small plants with fewer annual species than habitat (a). Habitat (c) is scrub dominated by shrub or small tree species such as hawthorn (*Crataegus* sp.). Finally, habitat (d) is woodland containing large, mature trees of species such as oak or beech. This is the end-point of the secondary succession and is referred to as the **climax community**.

▷ The early stages of a secondary succession are moved through more rapidly than those of a primary succession. Why do you think this is so?

▶ There is likely to be a greater availability of plant nutrients in the early stages of a secondary succession. There may also be seed already within the soil which can germinate rapidly. In the primary succession, seed has to arrive from *outside* the area. ■

(a)

(b)

(c)

(d)

Figure 5.1 These four habitats, (a) bare earth with annual plants, (b) grassland, (c) scrub, and (d) woodland, could be part of a secondary successional sequence in the same area. The alphabetical order of the habitats corresponds to the order of stages in the hypothetical succession, but they are not drawn to the same scale.

This chapter will be mainly concerned with secondary succession and, in particular, with a key problem that habitat management has to address—how to hold secondary succession in check. Frequently the management required is very simple and may appear crude, such as 'scrub-bashing', i.e. removing scrub to retain a grassland habitat. Similarly, use of grazing stock can keep potentially dominant grasses down and stop invasion by tree seedlings. (Recall the example of mowing the lawn in Section 2.1.2—this is a method of management which stops coarse grasses and woody species invading and thereby stops secondary succession.)

More is now understood about the ecological principles underlying succession and the requirements of the particular species to be managed. This has led to management techniques becoming increasingly refined. To illustrate this relationship between increased scientific knowledge and development of more sophisticated management techniques, we will look at one habitat which is managed for different groups of species.

5.2 Management of a habitat: chalk grassland

The chalk grasslands of England, such as those on the North and South Downs (Figure 5.2), are known to be amongst the richest habitats in Britain in terms of numbers of plant species. The vegetation of these areas 4 000 years ago was mature woodland (Section 2.2.2).

In the absence of management, grassland on chalk will revert back to woodland because of secondary succession. This was seen in a 'natural experiment' that occurred in the 1950s. To understand this natural experiment and the particular form of management it reveals, it is necessary to consider the effect that rabbits have on vegetation on the chalk and elsewhere.

5.2.1 Rabbits as agents of vegetation change

Rabbits have for many years been considered as agents of vegetation change. Their effects on vegetation are summarized in Extract 5.1 which is from the introduction to a scientific paper.

Before you read the extract, note that Breckland is a large area of open grassland on sandy and chalky soils in East Anglia. *Suaeda fruticosa* is now known as *Suaeda vera* or shrubby seablite, *Calluna vulgaris* is a heather, and *Carex arenaria* is a sedge (similar to a grass).

Extract 5.1   From A. S. Thomas, *Journal of Ecology* (1960) **48**, pp. 287–306.

Figure 5.2   Distribution of chalk in Great Britain. The North and South Downs are marked N and S, respectively.

Since 1900, there have been many studies of the influence of rabbit grazing on wild vegetation in Britain. One of the earliest accounts is by Wallis in *The Natural History of Cambridgeshire* (Marr and Shipley, 1904). Wallis described how the rabbits influenced the vegetation of Breckland, both by eating and by burrowing, and mentions some of the annual plants which grow on the soil disturbed by rabbits.

Oliver (1913) and Rowan (1913) described the feeding habits of rabbits on Blakeney Point, and listed plant species which were most attacked. In some cases the leaves were eaten, in others the flowers, in others the rhizomes; and the branches of *Suaeda fruticosa* were bitten off.

Farrow (1913, 1917) carefully described and photographed the effects of rabbits on the vegetation of Breckland, showing how *Calluna vulgaris* was killed by grazing and replaced by heath of *Carex arenaria* and of grasses. Watt (1937) queried the importance attributed by Farrow to rabbits in determining the present aspect of the Breckland region.

Another notable study of the effects of rabbits on vegetation was that by Tansley and Adamson (1925) on the chalk of the South Downs, and in which were listed the plants eaten by rabbits, and the plants which were avoided by rabbits, and which therefore tended to increase when they were abundant. This study was extended by Hope-Simpson (1940).

Other notable studies of the effects of rabbits were those of Fenton (1940) on hill grazing in Scotland; of Phillips (1935) on a reseeded pasture in Wales; and Gillham (1955) on the island of Skokholm, where vegetation under an abundance of rabbits was contrasted with that of the ungrazed island of Grassholm.

A prolonged and detailed study of the effect of excluding rabbits from Breckland grassland by Watt (1957) recognizes the possible effects of using wire-netting enclosures, and shows that the change from grazed to ungrazed is not likely to follow a straight course when gains or losses are plotted against time.

Extract 5.1 introduces two important effects of rabbits:

1 The plants of some species are preferentially eaten, reducing their abundance in rabbit-grazed vegetation. Conversely, some plants are avoided by rabbits and so tend to increase when rabbits are abundant.

2 Rabbits create gaps in the vegetation ('soil disturbed by rabbits') within which annual plants may grow.

▷ As annual plants are characteristic of the early stages of secondary succession (see Box 5.1), what is the effect of rabbits on secondary succession?

▸ Rabbits, in creating conditions suitable for early successional plants, are slowing down or even stopping succession.

A third factor, not mentioned in Extract 5.1, is that rabbits, at suitable densities, will tend to reduce the height and quantity of the vegetation to a low level. This will have an adverse effect on some later successional plants, such as coarse perennial grasses and tree seedlings, which, because they are better competitors, eventually come to dominate the vegetation in the absence of grazing. Tree seedlings, which as adults will dominate later successional stages and whose growing points are not close to the ground, may be killed by grazing rabbits. Therefore, the overall effect of the rabbits on secondary succession is to keep it at a *false* climax (end-point), referred to as a **plagioclimax**.

▷ What is the *natural* climax community of most chalk grasslands?

▸ Woodland.

Plagioclimax communities on chalk grassland affected by rabbits are typified by very short clipped vegetation, scrape holes and few trees. Because no one plant species is able to dominate, the number of plant species per unit area may be very high, perhaps 30–40 species in $1\,m^2$. We might therefore consider rabbits as a potential management tool for maintaining chalk grassland, creating conditions suitable for high numbers of plant species and favouring early successional plant species which otherwise might be quite rare. Convincing evidence of the effect of rabbits came in the 1950s when the rabbit population in Britain suffered a major decline, as revealed in Extract 5.2, which you should read now.

Extract 5.2   From A. Tittensor, *Country Life*, 3 February 1983.

Myxomatosis became familiar to most of us three decades ago when it swept rapidly through our rabbit populations, reducing them to a mere remnant of their former abundance. It is still with us, but both rabbit and disease have adapted to meet changing circumstances, and a temporary balance has been reached.

Myxomatosis is caused by the myxoma virus, and first caught the attention of scientists in 1896 when a stock of domestic laboratory rabbits in Montevideo was almost eliminated by an outbreak of the disease.

The introduction of myxomatosis to Europe and Australasia in order to reduce rabbit numbers was suggested as early as 1918, and field trials were started in the mid-1930s. There was, for example, an unsuccessful series of experiments on the Welsh island of Skokholm between 1936 and 1938. These early trials failed because the importance of blood-sucking insects, particularly fleas and mosquitoes, in transmitting the disease was not appreciated until later. It was subsequently discovered that virus particles are transferred on the insects' mouthparts from infected rabbit to new host. We now know that Skokholm was an unfortunate choice for such experiments, since it is the only known place in Britain where rabbits have no fleas.

Myxomatosis reached Europe in June 1952, when a retired doctor released two rabbits inoculated with virus on his sporting estate near Chartres in France. The estate was walled in, so it was anticipated that the disease would be confined to the site of introduction. However, it reached the Channel coast in December 1952, extended to southern France by June 1953, and had reached much of western Europe by the end of 1953. Myxomatosis crossed the Channel to an estate near Edenbridge in Kent during 1953, and had spread through much of south-eastern England by the following February, despite government efforts to eradicate it at source. Within two years the disease had reached most parts of Britain.

▷   How is the myxomatosis virus transmitted from rabbit to rabbit?

▸   By rabbit fleas and other blood-sucking insects.

The resultant effect on the vegetation, following the crash in rabbit numbers was dramatic, as revealed in the 'Discussion' section of A. S. Thomas' 1960 paper, part of which is reproduced here as Extract 5.3. (It may be useful to remind yourself of the contents of the earlier part of Thomas' paper in Extract 5.1 before reading Extract 5.3.)

In Extract 5.3, note that Kingley Vale, Old Winchester Hill and Pewsey Vale all contain chalk grassland habitats, and *Juniperus* and *Taxus* are the genera of juniper and yew. *Crataegus monogyna* is hawthorn, *Atropa belladonna* is deadly nightshade, *Cynoglossum officinale* is hound's-tongue, and *Senecio jacobaea* is ragwort. Some of these plant species are illustrated in Plate 5.2.

Extract 5.3   From A. S. Thomas (1960) *Journal of Ecology*, **48**, pp. 287–306.

Discussion

Spectacular changes in vegetation since the death of the rabbit have been reported from other countries: Australia (Ratcliffe, 1956), France (Morel, 1956), and the Netherlands (van Leeuwen, 1956). In the main, the changes reported in this paper were similar to those found in other countries, especially in the better regeneration of woody plants.

The bad influence of the rabbits in damaging and killing planted trees has long been known to foresters, and great expense has been incurred to erect rabbit-proof fences. But the localized influence of rabbits only becomes obvious in the course of this work, for it has determined the present aspect of some Nature Reserves. For example, Watt (1926) carefully mapped Kingley Vale, showing areas of *Juniperus* and *Taxus* scrub; he noticed that the rabbits grazed both *Juniperus* and *Taxus* and thought that their selective action benefited *Juniperus*. But these areas are now almost pure *Taxus* scrub, scarcely a *Juniperus* plant remaining. It has been noticed that large bushes of *Juniperus* tended to die back in the presence of rabbits, even though their bark was not eaten and their young shoots were above reach of the animals. As mentioned above, after the rabbits died many young *Juniperus* bushes became evident in the grassland, and it may be that this plant will become common again in the south of England.

Crataegus monogyna also was greatly curtailed by rabbits. For example, around the warren near the northern corner of the Old Winchester Hill Nature Reserve, there were few small *Crataegus* bushes and many *Taxus* bushes; but on the south-west side of the reserve, where rabbits were much fewer, dense *Crataegus* scrub had grown up. Therefore it is likely that, where the grazing influence of rabbits is not replaced by the grazing influence of sheep and cattle, scrub of *Crataegus* and other shrubs and trees may rapidly colonize much of the downlands.

Observers in other countries have emphasized the increase in various plants since the death of the rabbits, but few have reported such a decrease as shown by field notes on some of the transects in the south of England. It is only to be expected that plants encouraged by rabbits have become fewer; that will be a boon to farmers because many of these plants, such as *Atropa belladonna* and *Cynoglossum officinale*, are poisonous to stock.

Senecio jacobaea undoubtedly was encouraged by rabbits, who exposed and disturbed the soil by grazing and scratching, enabling the plant to become established. Although rabbits were generally considered to avoid *S. jacobaea* (Harper and Wood, 1957) yet it was observed in several places still infested by rabbits in 1954 that they prevented some *S. jacobaea* plants from fruiting, for they gnawed and felled the flowering stems, but ate little of them. After the rabbits died in 1954 and 1955 there was a spectacular display of flowering *S. jacobaea*. Colour photographs of the Pewsey Vale escarpment in Wiltshire showed patches of *S. jacobaea* only on rabbit burys in 1954, but a sheet of yellow flowers over the hillsides in 1955; in 1956 scarcely a single plant of *S. jacobaea* flowered there; in 1957 there were few plants in flower, again on the burys.

Question 5.1 With reference to Extract 5.3:

(a) What other grazers might be used as management tools for chalk grassland? Why do you think these would be better than rabbits?

(b) Which plant species *increased* after the decline of rabbit grazing?

(c) Which plant species *decreased* after the decline of the rabbit, and why?

The decline in rabbit numbers due to myxomatosis has revealed how the rabbit population had been affecting the composition and structure of the natural vegetation. By reducing the rabbits to a low density, a 'natural experiment' had occurred that demonstrated the effect of these grazers on vegetation. It also revealed the rabbits' efficacy, and potentially that of other grazers, as management tools for chalk grassland.

An interesting dilemma for conservation is posed by this result. Juniper, a native and uncommon plant in need of conservation, seemed to thrive after rabbit grazing declined. So, if management such as grazing, which can increase plant species richness, is implemented, it may be done at the expense of species such as juniper. In other words, the increase in numbers of plant species is *selective* in favour of certain early successional species. Similarly, if large numbers of plants in flower are desired, intensive uninterrupted grazing may not give the required result.

These dilemmas are frequent whenever management options are considered. In the following section, the management options within a grassland system are discussed in more detail.

5.2.2 The relative merits of different grassland types

This section will initially concentrate on one plant species which, over the last 20 years has come to dominate certain areas of formerly (plant) species-rich chalk grassland. The plant is a grass species, *Brachypodium pinnatum* (tor grass), which is an aggressive colonizer, outcompeting other grass and small plant species. Various reasons, including reduced grazing, have been put forward for the increase of tor grass in chalk grassland in Britain and mainland Europe, with much of the management of chalk grassland in southern England having been aimed at reducing its abundance and spread. It has been found that cattle grazing is most effective for achieving this reduction, although the grazing must not be too heavy and must be implemented only at certain times of year. Sheep grazing is apparently not suitable as the animals nibble around the tor grass, possibly even increasing its rate of spread.

Because plant communities dominated by tor grass are species-poor, i.e. have few different species present, the presence of the grass is generally considered to be a bad thing. In the light of this, read Extract 5.4, which is the abstract from a scientific paper. Remember that in concentrating on this summary you are following the habits of many readers looking for the key points in a scientific paper. Before you read the extract, note that a 'closed population' is one in which there is no immigration from or emigration to other populations. The butterfly's 'historical range' is its geographical range prior to the influence of humans.

Extract 5.4 From J. A. Thomas, *Ecological Entomology* (1983) **8**, pp. 427–435.

Abstract

1 A survey was made of the local butterfly, the Lulworth skipper (*Thymelicus acteon* Rott.) in Britain. Adult numbers were estimated on most sites and the habitat was analysed. Changes in numbers were also recorded in five populations over 6 years, and some aspects of behaviour were studied.

2 *T. acteon* forms closed populations. It was found in great abundance throughout its historical range, and appears both to have increased in numbers and to have spread locally. It has not extended its range.

3 The wrong larval foodplant is quoted by some modern textbooks. *T. acteon* requires mature *Brachypodium pinnatum* Beauv. plants for breeding. Within its range, the butterfly was almost ubiquitous in areas with tall *Brachypodium*.

4 The present abundance and probable increase of *T. acteon* is attributed to the spread of *B. pinnatum* in unimproved calcareous grassland. This has occurred through a decline in grazing, both by domestic stock and, since myxomatosis, by rabbits.

▷ What important link between the invasive tor grass (*Brachypodium pinnatum*) and the Lulworth skipper (*Thymelicus acteon*) was determined by J. A. Thomas' study (Extract 5.4)?

▶ Tor grass is the foodplant of the butterfly larva!

Extract 5.4 also confirms our ideas about the role of grazing management in that the spread of tor grass, and therefore the Lulworth skipper, was attributed to a decline in grazing by domestic stock and rabbits.

The requirement for grazing in chalk grassland management is provided by a second study of Thomas' on the Adonis blue butterfly (*Lysandra bellargus*). (You may recall the population size information given in Table 4.1 on the closely related chalkhill blue—the two species are in the same genus, *Lysandra*.) Again the summary of the original paper is provided, as Extract 5.5.

Extract 5.5   From J. A. Thomas (1983) *Journal of Applied Ecology*, **20**, pp. 59–83.

Summary

1   The ecology and status of the declining butterfly, *Lysandra bellargus*, were studied by recording the behaviour of all stages of the life cycle; by monitoring adult population changes on seven sites; and from surveys and habitat analyses of former and existing colonies.

2   *L. bellargus* forms local closed populations that fly in small discrete areas. It reaches its northern limit in Britain, and breeds mainly on south-facing slopes in the extreme south, although its foodplant, *Hippocrepis comosa*, is common in most calcareous grassland.

3   The larvae are tended incessantly by ants after their first instar. Ants also tend pupae, which occur inside their nests or are buried in earth cells.

4   Egg-laying is virtually restricted to *H. comosa* growing in a 1–4 cm tall sward [area of grassland], perhaps because these situations are warm and support many ants. Monitored populations were larger when their sites were closely-cropped, although very heavy grazing was harmful. No colony was found on a former site whose sward had grown above a mean height of 5 cm.

5   The number of *L. bellargus* colonies in Britain has halved every 12 years since the early 1950s. Perhaps 70–80 populations survive, of which most are small.

6   Most (perhaps all) extinctions were due to habitat change. About one third resulted from the loss of *H. comosa*, mainly through ploughing or agricultural improvement. All other former sites support an abundance of foodplant, but few are sufficiently well grazed nowadays to support *L. bellargus*. Butterfly collectors, colony isolation, and bad weather are unlikely to have been important factors in the decline.

7   It is often uneconomic to graze unimproved grassland adequately for *L. bellargus*. Nor, since myxomatosis, have unstocked sites been maintained by rabbits. It is predicted that most remaining colonies will become extinct unless conservation bodies intervene. Past measures have proved inadequate, and new advice is given in this paper.

▷   What are the ecological requirements of the Adonis blue butterfly?

▸   Availability of the larval foodplant (*Hippocrepis comosa*), with a *short* sward (1–4 cm high), the presence and abundance of ants, and a preference for south-facing slopes.

▷   What is the main cause of the decline of the Adonis blue butterfly?

▸   Habitat change resulting from ploughing, 'improvement' (fertilizing) of grassland, and inadequate levels of grazing. Note that unimproved grassland is often uneconomic to stock with cattle or sheep. The situation has been made worse (from the butterfly's point of view) by the decline of the natural grazer, the rabbit, due to myxomatosis.

▷   How can the decline in the Adonis blue butterfly be overcome?

▸   By managing the grassland, for example through higher grazing—although this is difficult and, as noted above, may not be economically viable.

Not all the details of the management possibilities are given in the summary. One of the other possibilities mentioned by Thomas in his discussion is creating 'scattered south-facing sun-spots'. This would involve creating large gaps in the vegetation which, as Thomas noted, 'could easily be achieved using explosives'!

In summary, there appear to be advantages to different types of grassland, indicating that grassland is not really a single habitat but is composed of several types of habitat. Some insect species need long grass for protection from predators or for feeding, whilst other insect species require very short turf. Similarly, requirements of flowering plant species, small mammals or snails reveal conflicting management priorities within grassland areas. The best management may be that which is aimed at producing mosaics of long and short grass—a simple formula that is difficult (or at least requires sizeable inputs of labour and time) to achieve in practice.

It is important that management proceeds hand-in-hand with monitoring of the population size, as illustrated in Section 4.2. Indeed, a continual interaction between habitat (or more rarely, species) management and population assessment is required, as the latter is the measure of success of the former.

Summary of Chapter 5

1   Habitat management often involves the control of secondary succession, for example slowing down or stopping succession at a false endpoint.

2   The study of the rabbit in Britain during the 20th century has revealed the potential for chalk grassland management by grazing animals.

3   Grassland is a composite habitat, in which areas of long and short grass may occur, favouring different species of insect and plant.

Activity 5.1   *You should spend up to 1 hour on this activity.*

In this activity, a different habitat from lowland chalk grassland is considered, together with a different form of management from grazing. The habitat is heather moorland and blanket bog, which is found in many upland areas of Britain. The heather is a mixture of *Calluna vulgaris* and various *Erica* species, whilst bogs are characterized by the presence of *Sphagnum* moss species.

Extract 5.6 discusses a conference held in 1989 that considered the population dynamics of the red grouse. This is a review article, bringing together a range of (conflicting) views from different research groups, and is written in a rather more accessible style than the formal scientific publications studied earlier. The extract is of particular value in the present context in that it touches on ideas of population dynamics, notably density dependence, from Chapter 4, on the issues of animal harvesting (Chapter 3), and on some of the dilemmas and difficulties of habitat management mentioned in the present chapter.

Now read the extract carefully, following whatever reading strategy you have found works best to help your concentration. Do not attempt to understand every detail described (the last two paragraphs contain some complex ideas) but try to identify and remember, or make notes on what you judge to be the key points. Test your recollection of the points made in the article by answering (a)–(g); only look back at the extract or your notes if you need to.

(a) What is the alternative land use to grouse shooting in open moorland?

(b) Why is moorland that is managed for grouse populations occasionally burnt?

(c) State briefly the views of the Institute of Terrestrial Ecology (ITE) and the Game Conservancy (GC) on the population dynamics of grouse, in each case in no more than 50 words.

(d) Give at least one item of evidence in support of each of the opposing points of view in (c).

(e) Explain the meaning of the term 'delayed density dependence'.

(f) Provide an answer, in no more than 100 words, on how loss and degradation of habitat contribute to the decline in size of the grouse population.

(g) Is there any evidence against the 'compromise' proposal that some of the changes in some grouse populations are the consequence of worm infections, others are a consequence of changes in breeding behaviour and success, and others due to habitat degradation?

Extract 5.6   From *Nature* (1990) **343**, 25 January, pp. 310–311.

The moorland owners' grouse

John R. Krebs and Robert M. May

The red grouse *Lagopus lagopus scoticus* is more than a 600 gramme member of the family Galliformes. It plays a central, if somewhat self-sacrificial, role in the grouse-shooting enterprise in Britain; an average of 400 000 grouse are shot each year and they generate a gross income of the order of £10 million. The economic rewards from grouse shooting and its associated industries are by no means negligible for those living in many rural communities of northern England and Scotland, but for many outside these areas the conservation issues related to grouse-shooting are of even greater importance. There are roughly one million hectares of grouse-shooting land in Britain, primarily heather moorland and blanket bog; these habitats are rare and becoming rarer on a national and Western European scale and they support an unusual flora and fauna. The conservation issue can be stated simply: if grouse-shooting cannot be made to pay (this requires a summer grouse density of about 140 birds km^{-2} and a concomitant bag of around 35 birds km^{-2}) the main alternative form of land use for these upland areas is forestry. Silent, gloomy ranks of Sitka spruce replace open moorland and the characteristic plants, insects, birds and mammals disappear. Sadly for the cause of conservation, and for those who make their living from grouse shooting, stocks of grouse appear to be diminishing. This was the background to a recent workshop, the aim of which was to assess current knowledge about the dynamics of red grouse populations and the implications of this knowledge for harvesting and management.

Scientists from two research groups were brought together to discuss their results with experts from Britain and North America. One group, based at Banchory near Aberdeen, is part of the Institute of Terrestrial Ecology (ITE) and has been studying red grouse popu-lations in north-east Scotland since 1956. The other, from the Game Conservancy (GC), has been studying the red grouse in northern England since 1979 and in Scotland since 1985. The two groups broadly agree on the demographic facts about red grouse popu-lations, but they offer different views on why grouse numbers change and hence on how to manage grouse populations in order to main-tain or improve yields.

Three potentially independent demographic patterns were accepted by both teams as being unequivocal. First, since the beginning of the twentieth century there has been a gradual long-term decline in the number of grouse shot both in England and Scotland. In Scotland, the decline was particularly marked in the period preceding and during the Second World War and again in the 1970s and 1980s (see figure). Second, different moors characteristically support different average densities of grouse; for example, heather moor in Scotland has a higher density of grouse than moorland covered by peat bog in Ireland. Third, and perhaps most intriguing, in many—but not all—moors, grouse show cyclic oscillations in numbers, with peaks occurring every 4 years (northern England) or every 6 years (Scotland). These cycles appear to be roughly synchronized over wide areas.

Both the ITE and GC groups agreed that the long-term decline in grouse is associated with habitat degradation. A combination of over-grazing by sheep and deer, improvement of uplands by drainage and the development of forestry has led to a decrease in the extent and quality of heather moorland, the grouse's pre-ferred habitat and main source of food (young heather shoots). The effects of habitat degra-dation may be exacerbated by a concomitant increase in habitats for predators on grouse. Furthermore, management of both predator populations and extant heather moorland by gamekeepers is not as intensive as it was in the earlier part of this century.

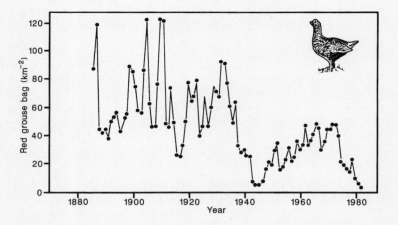

Number of grouse shot per square kilometre in the Scottish Highlands over the past 100 years. Note the long-term decline; the relatively large declines around the two world wars; and the roughly cyclic changes within the longer term trends.

Differences between moors in average population density may also be related, at least in part, to differences in vegetation structure. In general, moors that are less productive for grouse have little heather and often overlie acidic rocks, whereas productive moors have plenty of heather and overlie basic rocks. Thus it might, to some extent, be possible both to halt the decline of grouse populations and increase the productivity of poor moors by replanting heather or encouraging its regrowth (government grants are now available for this) and by managing the heather carefully once it is established. Careful management in this context means burning small strips of the heather on a rotational basis so that the moorland consists of a fine-scale patchwork of young heather, which is nutritious and provides good food, and old heather which provides cover for the grouse.

The causes of cycles in grouse numbers are more enigmatic and here the two groups place emphasis on different causes. Four broad kinds of explanations were discussed at the meeting: behavioural changes associated with changes in average territory size, and interactions between red grouse and their parasites, their predators and their food supply. The essential feature of any hypothesis for cycles is that it must incorporate effects that exert 'delayed density-dependence' on grouse populations. This simply means that, as grouse numbers go up, the severity of the effects that depress recruitment or increase mortality must increase with a lag and then remain high long enough after the grouse have started to decline to sustain the decline for more than one season.

It is easy to understand why parasites might act in this manner. If their effect on grouse depends both on transmission rate (likely to be related to grouse density) and on the intensity of infection, then disease will become more common (with a slight lag) as grouse density increases and will remain high after it has started to cause decline in grouse numbers. This idea was first proposed by James Dalziell Dougal in 1875, in a report on a decline in grouse numbers during the 1860s and 1870s. The GC view is that a gut helminth, *Trichostrongylus tenuis*, causes fluctuations in grouse numbers primarily by reducing recruitment to the population through its effect on chick survival.

The evidence for this view is threefold. First, a ten-year study of Gunnerside Moor in North Yorkshire showed that both grouse and helminths show cyclic variations in their numbers. Second, populations to the west of the Pennines tend to be cyclic and to have high parasite loads, whereas those on the eastern side of the Pennines are less cyclic and have lower parasite loads. It is thought that this difference relates to rainfall: conditions on the wet western moors are more favourable for the survival of free-living stages of the parasite than are the drier conditions in the east. Third, experimental treatment of female grouse with an anti-helminthic drug increased their production of young and perhaps their survival (a result also obtained by the ITE group). It is not, however, straightforward to translate this evidence into the conclusion that helminths cause grouse cycles. The descriptive data do not disentangle cause and effect, and it is not yet clear whether the experimentally induced effects on chick survival are sufficient to drive the cycle. As a test of the hypothesis, P. J. Hudson has developed a method of coating grit, which is eaten by the grouse, with an anti-helminth drug and has persuaded two land-owners in North Yorkshire to treat their entire moors with the coated grit. The cyclic decline in grouse numbers on the two treated moors was less marked than on untreated, nearby, controls, but it is still too early to say whether or not the treatment will actually prevent population cycles.

The ITE team, whilst acknowledging that parasites may affect production of grouse chicks, emphasizes the importance of behavioural changes in territorial grouse as a cause of cycles. By removing territorial cocks and associated hens, the team has shown that in many years (especially years of high density) territorial behaviour in the autumn determines the number of breeders in the following spring. Many birds are evicted from the moorland by territory owners and these individuals often die or disappear from the local population. Crucial for translating this behavioural mechanism of limitation of breeding density into one that causes cycles is to propose a mechanism whereby territory size changes from one year to the next in a delayed density-dependent fashion. Here, the ITE team does not have any critical evidence, although it has some intriguing results from captive birds suggesting that relative aggressiveness changes from year to year and that the birds hatching from eggs laid in high-density populations are more tolerant than those hatching from eggs in low-density populations.

The ITE group had originally favoured the view that cycling within a moor may be related to changes in heather quality. But attempts to halt a cyclic decline in the 1970s by fertilizing heather failed, and the team has therefore rejected the idea of a plant–herbivore interaction as the cause of the cycle. But it was felt by the workshop that this hypothesis should not be ruled out altogether.

Finally, both groups agreed that predators such as foxes, crows and raptors are not likely to be the cause of cycles in grouse populations, because predators do not seem to be sufficiently abundant to cause grouse numbers to decline from the peak of the cycle. There was, however, some discussion of the possibilities that predators may have an effect on average grouse numbers and that they may keep them down when the population is already low for other reasons. Especially delicate, in this context, is the suggestion by the GC workers that predation by hen harriers prevent grouse populations from increasing (and both groups emphatically agreed that it is premature to jump to this conclusion) conservationists would be presented with a 'Catch 22' situation—the conservation of heather moors and their unusual fauna and flora depends on increasing grouse stocks; but the simple-minded way to increase grouse stocks would be to remove hen harriers, one of the species for which the moor is being conserved.

Even if we had a clear understanding of the dynamics of red grouse populations in general, and of the mechanism causing cycles in particular, there would still remain questions about how best to harvest grouse. Among other things, the answer depends on whether the aim is to maximize average yield or to reduce fluctuations in yields by eliminating cycles. These aims may conflict: for a population that is naturally cyclic, it can be shown that average yields are often maximized by a level of harvesting that leaves the population cycling (albeit with modified amplitude, period or both). Levels of harvesting that are high enough to suppress cycling may be beyond the so-called 'maximum sustained yield' (MSY) point, resulting in relatively steady yields but at a lower level. A more general issue is that harvesting will often affect a population's ability to withstand the effects of unpredictable environmental perturbations, so that variance in yield becomes relatively larger as the MSY point is approached. In short, various kinds of trade-offs must be weighed against each other in any harvesting plan.

Whatever the harvesting policy, there remains the question of moorland management. Because landowners already manage moors, it might be possible to advance our understanding by treating management as a deliberate experiment. It would be interesting, for example, to compare the outcomes of a factorial experiment in which different moors were either treated or not treated with anti-helminth drugs and where the heather was or was not subjected to traditional patchwork burning. Such management-as-experiment could both produce insights into fundamental ecological questions and help to secure the future of grouse moorlands.

6 Biological diversity

Biological diversity (or **biodiversity**) is a concept that includes the whole array of life-forms and their components, from genes through species to habitats and ecosystems. (The ecosystem is defined as all the living and non-living components, e.g. water and nutrients, in a particular area.) More specifically, it is a measure of the richness and evenness in composition of the units of an ecological system. An **ecological community** is defined as being composed of individuals of different species; a community with *high* biological diversity is one that has about equal numbers of individuals (high evenness) of many different species (high **species richness**). It is not the total number of individuals that is important in determining species diversity but rather the relative proportions of individuals of each species and the number of species. There are several different types of **diversity index**, each of which aims to summarize the diversity of a community (or other ecological system) in a single value. In the following example, one of the simpler measures of diversity, the Simpson index, will be used.

6.1 The Simpson diversity index

The **Simpson diversity index** has the attractive property that the maximum theoretical value (highest diversity) is very close to one (although it can never equal one) and the minimum theoretical value is zero. To calculate the Simpson diversity index for any community we need to know the number (or biomass) of individuals of each species in that community. We then calculate the proportion of the total number of individuals contributed by each species. For example, if there are 30 individuals in an area and 10 of these are species A, then the proportion of A individuals is 10/30 or 1/3. The proportion for each species is then squared, the squared values are totalled and the total subtracted from 1 to give the Simpson index value. The following examples should make these calculations clearer and illustrate what determines whether a community has a high or low diversity.

Let us begin by considering a community made up of four species, each with ten individuals, in Table 6.1:

Table 6.1

Species	Number of individuals	Proportion	(Proportion)^2
A	10	1/4	1/16
B	10	1/4	1/16
C	10	1/4	1/16
D	10	1/4	1/16
total	40	1	1/4
1 − total			3/4 = 0.75

So this community of four species has a Simpson diversity index of 0.75. Now compare this result with that obtained by keeping the same total number of individuals in equal proportions but doubling the number of species, in Table 6.2.

Table 6.2

Species	Number of individuals	Proportion	(Proportion)^2
A	5	1/8	1/64
B	5	1/8	1/64
C	5	1/8	1/64
D	5	1/8	1/64
E	5	1/8	1/64
F	5	1/8	1/64
G	5	1/8	1/64
H	5	1/8	1/64
total	40	1	8/64 = 1/8
1 − total			7/8 = 0.875

The Simpson diversity index value has increased from 0.75 to 0.875.

Now let us return to a four-species community with 40 individuals, except that this time the distribution of individuals is different between species (Table 6.3). In this case, species A is *dominant*.

Table 6.3

Species	Number	Proportion	(Proportion)^2
A	28	28/40 = 0.7	0.49
B	4	4/40 = 0.1	0.01
C	4	4/40 = 0.1	0.01
D	4	4/40 = 0.1	0.01
total	40	1	0.52
1 − total			0.48

▷ What has been the effect of altering the proportions away from equal values for the community of four species?

▶ It has *reduced* the Simpson diversity index from 0.75 (Table 6.1) to 0.48.

▷ What is the relationship between dominance and diversity revealed in this example?

▶ Dominance is *inversely* related to diversity.

→ more species without a principle dominance = larger Simpson diversity index.

These examples show that high Simpson diversity index values are produced by higher numbers of species and a more even spread of individuals between species. Of course, the ability to quantify diversity is quite different from understanding *why* a particular community is highly diverse. This is a problem with which ecologists have grappled for many years and its discussion is largely beyond the scope of this book, although we have seen the importance of factors such as grazing in maintaining a high diversity of plant species in chalk grassland (Chapter 5).

You need to be aware that when diversity values for many ecological communities are given, particularly in the popular literature on biological conservation, several simplifications are adopted. Two of these are identified in Activity 6.1.

Activity 6.1

Extract 6.1 by Tim Radford was written at the time of the biodiversity convention, which was signed by most countries at the 'Earth Summit' in Rio de Janeiro in June 1992, and is aimed at the interested layperson who may have little background knowledge of the subject. Such an article should attempt to strike a balance between grabbing the attention of the reader and providing a simplified yet accurate account of the science. Read Extract 6.1 and then answer the following questions.

(a) In general, is the article written in a scientifically accurate way? In particular, does the definition of biodiversity agree with the one used in this chapter?

(b) One simplification in the use of biodiversity, hinted at in the article, is that diversity measures are often based on a selective sample of species within an area: one rarely (if ever) considers the total biodiversity of an area. What part of the extract implies that biodiversity estimates are selective?

Extract 6.1 From *The Guardian*, 6 June 1992.

Healing force of evolution

Tim Radford on the life-saving properties of plants and small creatures

Biodiversity is the jargon word for everything that lives on the planet. Since Carl Linnaeus started classifying life in the 18th century, biologists have described, named, and identified about 1.8 million species, and conjectured that there might be 2 or 3 million.

Only in the past 10 years have they begun to realise that the mangrove swamps, the coral reefs, the ocean floors, and the tropical rainforests are unimaginably rich and various in plant and insect life.

The guess is that there might be between 8 and 80 million species, and this does not count microbes or fungi. The guess is that half of all of them could be extinct in the next century.

All crop plants benefit from genes taken from their wild cousins and ancestors. The pharmaceutical industry rests heavily on wild 'chemical factories' designed by millions of years of evolution.

For instance American scientists at the National Institute of Health have extracted from the skin of an Ecuadorian frog a chemical which turns out to be a painkiller 200 times more potent than morphine.

Snails and slugs have some curious properties, too. 'They live in an environment absolutely crammed with pathogens, bacteria, and fungi' says Professor John Lawton, a population biologist.

'It turns out they have absolutely fascinating antibiotics in their mucus. And there is a huge amount of interest in certain Japanese pharmaceutical companies in identifying what those antibiotics are and how they work.'

The Madagascar rosy periwinkle turned out to have produced for itself not one but two anti-cancer drugs: these are now worth £111 million a year. The US National Cancer Institute is screening thousands of plants a year.

Twenty-five per cent of prescription drugs contain products derived from plants. Nobody knows exactly why the willow tree decided to produce aspirin in its bark, why one family of drugs from the paw-paw has powerful cytotoxic, anti-cancer or anti-malaria properties, or why the Pacific yew should produce quantities of taxol, now an important anti-cancer drug.

Jared Diamond, another population biologist who recently won the £10 000 Rhone-Poulenc science book prize for his *The Rise and Fall of the Third Chimpanzee*, argues that every plant produces secondary compounds 'because every plant risks being eaten by some animal. That right away guarantees that these compounds are biologically active.'

In the chemical warfare arms race between plant and insect the weaponry becomes enormously sophisticated. The neem tree uses azadirachtin in ways which—if a human developed it—would seem morally appalling: by suppressing insect appetites and stunting sexual development.

(handwritten) roughly compares to known fact, so reasonably safe to assume the rest of the article is fairly accurate

(handwritten) very high!

Not all plant chemicals convert to medicines. One Amazon tree—slower to grow, at a disadvantage in the competition for light—uses the crudest means to protect itself from insect attack.

At the first bite it exudes a sticky substance which simply cements the predator's jaws so that it will never bite again. It is, of course, the plant that makes the world go round: rubber.

6.2 Quantifying world biodiversity and its loss

As you know by now, the term 'species richness' refers to one component of diversity, that of the number of species; you also know that species diversity is greatest in the tropics. So, comparing habitat for habitat, we would expect, for example, temperate forest to have a lower species richness of trees, insects, mammals, birds etc., than tropical forests. Similarly, we expect aquatic habitats to have higher richness in the tropics. However, there are exceptions: some of the most species-rich areas in the oceans are at high latitudes because of the upwelling currents. Similarly, some insect groups are reputed to be most diverse at mid-latitudes, e.g. ichneumonids, a group of parasitic wasps. However, for many groups of species, there is indeed a gradient of species richness with changing latitude (Figure 6.1).

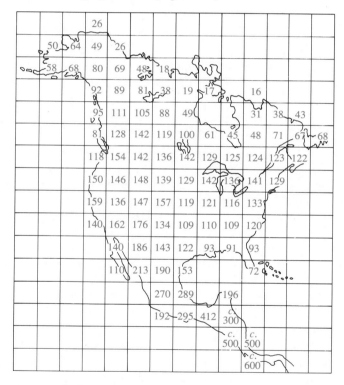

Figure 6.1 An example of a 'north–south' gradient of species richness in North America. The figures refer to the numbers of species of breeding birds in areas of equal size.

We referred to one particular aspect of species richness in Section 2.2.1; tropical Guyana had at least 15 times as many species of butterfly as temperate Britain. Question 2.3 highlighted an important assumption about the effects of deforestation.

▷ Can you recall that assumption?

▶ That deforestation would lead to extinction of species *in direct proportion* to the amount of habitat lost.

Sections 6.2.1 and 6.2.2 will analyse this assumption in more detail, as it helps us to understand how far conservation scientists have come in describing and quantifying the world's biodiversity. In these discussions on biodiversity we will continuously need to refer to the levels of classification of organisms. If you need to refresh your memory, some of the important principles are covered in Box 6.1.

6.1 | *Box 6.1   Classification of organisms*

We have seen that all organisms can be classified into different species. These species are themselves put into higher categories based on the overlap of their physical and chemical characteristics. We noted that the oak trees are in the genus *Quercus*. Genera are themselves put into families. For example, the family Fagaceae, within which oak trees are placed, includes sweet chestnut (*Castanea sativa*) and beech (*Fagus sylvatica*). The species are placed in this family because they have a series of common characteristics. In the case of plants these similarities are primarily with respect to flower and fruit structure. Families are themselves placed into orders, orders into classes, classes into phyla (singular phylum), and finally, phyla into kingdoms. The kingdom is the highest category within which organisms can be placed. All plants and animals are organized in this hierarchical **classification** system, with plants forming one kingdom and animals a second kingdom.

The process of identifying organisms so that they can be put into the correct categories at particular levels is called **taxonomy**. It is not important to commit to memory all the various levels into which organisms can be placed, nor to recall all the various categories within a level, for example, the different phyla in the animal kingdom. With use, you will become familiar with the levels and with *some* of the categories within a level, although the levels of family, genus and species contain so many representatives that even the most dedicated taxonomist can only ever recall a small fraction of them. In fact many taxonomists, perhaps working in the Royal Botanic Gardens at Kew or the Natural History Museum in South Kensington, devote themselves to studying just one or two families of plants or animals. ■

6.2.1 Quantifying insect diversity in tropical forest trees

Recording and mapping the world's biodiversity is an enormously complex and difficult task. Some of the most spectacular advances in the last decade have occurred in knowledge of the insects of the tropical forest (see Section 2.2.1). Insect species make up about 75% of all animal species, which means that knowledge of their species richness greatly helps the estimation of the total number of animal species in the world. The total numbers of species of vertebrates (other than fish) and flowering plants are fairly certain; a few more species might be discovered each year but these contribute little to the overall total number of species. In contrast, many hundreds of thousands or even millions of insect species await discovery and description. At present, about 10 000 new species (of any type of organism) are described each year, although approximately 3 000 are struck off the list annually as it is discovered that they have been described before under another name!

Insects (the class Insecta) are divided into 29 orders, of which the beetles (Coleoptera), moths and butterflies (Lepidoptera), true flies (Diptera), true bugs (Hemiptera), and bees, ants and wasps (Hymenoptera) are most numerous. The largest order of insects is Coleoptera, with about 400 000 described species world-wide. This prompted the famous quote from the biologist J. B. S. Haldane that what he could infer from his studies of natural history about the Creator was his 'inordinate fondness for beetles'.

This section will consider in detail the work in Brunei, Borneo of Nigel Stork of the British Natural History Museum. In 1982, he collected samples of insects from the canopies of ten tropical trees following the methods given in Extract 6.2. The full 'methods' section is given to provide you with a detailed impression of the problems that have to be overcome. You need not concern yourself with the fine details (e.g. the various tree species involved) but try to form a mental picture of how these data were painstakingly assembled!

Extract 6.2   From N. E. Stork (1991) *Journal of Tropical Ecology*, **7**, pp. 161–180.

Methods

Field site and tree selection

Ten trees were selected for fogging in an area of primary forest on the alluvial terrace south of the Sungai (River) Benutan near Bukit Sulang, Ladan Hills Forest Reserve (4° 42′ N, 114° 42′ E) in Brunei, Borneo (Figure 1). The forest had little ground level vegetation although the low canopy was dense and dominated by rotan palms. The canopy was of mixed levels up to 50 m with a few 'super-emergents' reaching heights of over 70 m.

During the fieldwork (29 August to 9 September 1982) there were several short periods of heavy rainfall. Some two weeks after the last fogging a period of several days of rain caused the field site to flood for at least several days up to a depth of more than a metre, confirming the view that this represented an area of typical lowland floodplain forest. Rainfall averages above 2 500 mm in this region with no distinct rainy season. Fogged trees were identified by Dr M. Huby (Table 1) and none appeared to be in flower or fruit.

Insecticide fogging procedure

A synthetic pyrethroid insecticide, Reslin E, was diluted 1 part to 49 parts of diesel (equivalent to 0.8% active ingredient) and applied to trees using a Swing Fog SN11 insecticide fogging machine. This was hauled into the canopy of each tree by a rope and pulley system erected in the tree the previous day using a

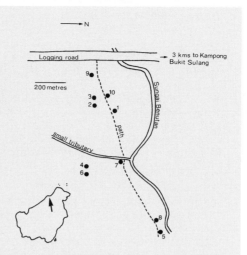

Figure 1   Map of study site near Bukit Sulang, Brunei. Filled circles represent positions of fogged trees. Inset: map of Borneo showing location of field site.

line-throwing gun. The insecticide has high knockdown and relatively low kill components which affect the nervous system of insects. The resulting agitated movements of the insects cause many to drop off leaves which may intercept their fall from the higher canopy. The insecticide is non-residual, breaking down in minutes in direct sunlight, and is non-toxic to vertebrates. Approximately 2.5 litres of the mixture were used per tree—sufficient to over-fog it.

Table 1   Data on the 10 Bornean trees sampled by insecticide fogging including tree height (ht.), canopy depth (can.), diameter of trunk at breast height or just above buttresses (dbh), estimates of percentage leaf cover above sample sheets (leaf) and epiphyte load on trees (epiph.) scaled from 4 (high) to 1 (almost no visible epiphytes). Linear measurements are in metres.

Tree species	No.	ht.	can.	dbh.	leaf	epiph.
Dipterocarpaceae: *Shorea johorensis* Foxwood	1	70	40	1.3	55	4
	2	72	32	1.2	35	4
	3	33	24	0.8	85	1
	4	55	30	1.0	40	1
Shorea macrophylla (De Vriese)	5	52	29	1.0	60	3
	6	56	40	1.5	55	2
Anacardiaceae: *Pentaspadon motleyi* Hook	7	29	12	0.5	55	1
	8	43	23	0.5	65	3
Fagaceae: *Castanopsis* sp.	9	35	21	0.5	65	1
Family and species indeterminate	10	27	17	0.4	70	1

Trees selected for sampling were fogged in pairs, one pair per day. Sufficient low vegetation was cleared to allow the placement of two plastic sheets, each 2.5×4 m, on the ground directly beneath the canopy of each tree immediately prior to fogging. The fog is warm and rises unless there is any sort of wind. Since in the tropics the calmest time of day is usually dawn, fogging was carried out at about 0600 h. In all cases, except for trees 1 and 2, insecticide fog reached the tops or near to the tops of the trees and there was little wind drift.

Most insects fell within the first 20 minutes of fogging but a two hour 'drop-time' was allowed before they were carefully brushed into the centre of the plastic sheets for transfer to pots containing 70% alcohol. Insecticide 'drop-time' has been analysed for British oak trees and the results will be published elsewhere (Stork and Hammond unpublished). Tree number 5 was refogged 10 days after its first fogging, with the sheets in the same positions as before.

Insecticide fogging collects mostly insects that are on the surface of leaves and branches and, although similar insecticides are commercially used to flush out cockroaches in buildings, many insects hidden in cracks or under bark may be missed. Leaf-miners and leaf-rollers are poorly sampled as are those insects firmly attached to the leaves such as mealybugs, some psyllid nymphs and possibly some aphids. Although no data are available on how well these and other concealed insects such as those in ant or termite nests are sampled, brief visual checks after insecticide fogging experiments in Britain and Sulawesi suggest that few insects are left on the leaves. Further investigations are required on the efficiency of insecticide sampling. The insecticide samples described here represent the arthropod fauna at one point in time and comparisons and conclusions drawn from them must be tempered by this limitation.

Sample preparation and sorting

Samples were sorted to Order and distributed to specialists within the Department of Entomology of The Natural History Museum. Most arthropods were sorted to species which were cross-referenced between the different samples so that the total number of species in the combined samples could be estimated. For Lepidoptera, Psocoptera, Nematocera and Brachycera (not Empididae) numbers of species were only roughly estimated. For these groups and for Braconidae, where the species were accurately sorted, samples were not cross-referenced and hence accurate *in toto* counts are not available. Acarina and Pseudoscorpiones were not sorted to species. Nymphs of Hemiptera (except Psylloidea) were not sorted but were apportioned to Homoptera and Heteroptera in the same ratio as the adults.

Activity 6.2

(a) Why do you think that the results of the work were only published in 1991, 9 years after collecting the data?

(b) Summarize the various steps involved in insect sampling and identification in a suitable way, e.g. using a numbered list, an annotated diagram or a flow chart.

As an example of the extraordinary biodiversity in the tree canopy we will consider the data on beetle species from the same ten trees as in Extract 6.2. As a point of reference it is helpful to know that there are about 4000 species of beetle (Coleoptera) in Britain covering about 95 families. As coleopterists have been active in Britain for many years, this is likely to be quite close to the real number of species.

Activity 6.3 *You should spend up to 1 hour on this activity.*

Using the data in Table 6.4, it is possible to calculate a Simpson diversity index. Up to now, such an index has indicated *species* diversity. However, in the present example the same arithmetical steps are followed, using the number of *species* in each *family*, rather than the number of individuals in each species. (We could also use the number of individuals in each family.)

(a) (i) Calculate the Simpson family diversity index for the data in Table 6.4.

(ii) What does the calculated value tell you? Do you think this value is a useful summary of these data?

A second method of summarizing the data is to plot a **rank–abundance curve**. In this graph, the number of species (or number of individuals) in each family is plotted on the vertical axis against rank (1 = most abundant (greatest number of species), 2 = second most abundant, and so on) of the family on the horizontal axis.

(b) (i) Plot the family rank–abundance curve using the number of species in each family from Table 6.4.

(ii) Describe the graph—what does it tell you about the data?

(iii) Where would the other 50 Coleoptera families be plotted if they were included in this graph? *Which would give a fairly flat curve.*

(c) How is the rank–abundance curve linked to the Simpson diversity index?

Now that we know something about the beetle families from the ten trees we can put this into the context of the insect fauna as a whole from those same ten trees (Table 6.5).

(d) Summarize the data in Table 6.5 in the form of a rank–abundance curve using the number of species in each order. Plot at least ten orders in this way, ignoring those orders with an unknown number of species. What conclusions can you draw from this graph?

Table 6.4 The ten most abundant Coleoptera (beetle) families (in terms of number of species) collected from ten trees in Brunei. A total of 60 Coleoptera families were recorded. The total number of species in these ten most abundant families is given.

Coleoptera families	No. of species	No. of individuals	
Pselaphidae	25	64	.044
Staphylinidae	115	501	.20
Elateridae	27	295	.05
Corylophidae	33	200	.06
Coccinellidae	20	46	.035
Aderidae	45	124	.08
Tenebrionidae	32	87	.056
Chrysomelidae	107	570	.19
Anthribidae	38	80	.067
Curculionidae	129	469	.23
total for ten families	571	2436	

Σc^2

1 .0019
2 .040
3 .002
4 .0033
5 .0012
6 .0062
7 .0031
8 .0351
9 .0044
10 .0610   Σ .1482

SDI = .85

Shows how the species are spread

Table 6.5 A summary of the numbers of species and individuals in all insect orders collected from ten trees in Brunei.

Order	No. of species	No. of individuals
Thysanura	?	26
Ephemeroptera	8	15
Odonata	4	4
Orthoptera	65	466
Blattodea	40	451
Dermaptera	5	48
Phasmida	11	26
Mantodea	5	10
Psocoptera	?	896
Hemiptera	269	2656
Thysanoptera	130	851
Neuroptera	7	21
Lepidoptera	50	626
Trichoptera	1	1
Diptera	444	5106
Coleoptera	859	4043
Hymenoptera	945	6644
Phthiraptera	1	1
total	2844	21891

?, unknown

As demonstrated by Table 6.5, the species richness of beetles is only one facet of the extraordinary diversity discovered to be harboured in these ten trees in Brunei. Indeed, you will probably have noticed from Table 6.5 that, in this sample, the Coleoptera were the *second* most species-rich insect order, following the Hymenoptera. Stork noted that:

> *The sheer diversity of these samples is perhaps best demonstrated by Chalcidoidea (parasitic Hymenoptera)—the 1455 specimens from the 10 fogged trees represent 739 species. To put these numbers into perspective, there are probably less than 100 species (previously) recorded from the whole of Borneo and less than 1500 species in Britain.*

6.2.2 Tropical deforestation: implications for insect diversity

Now that we have a feel for the size and range of insect diversity in the tropical forest canopy, let us return to the problem of the effects of deforestation on biodiversity. What would be the effect on biological diversity of cutting down the ten trees sampled by Stork? It is likely that there would be *no* reduction in species richness because representatives of those species will live elsewhere. What then about cutting down 100 trees, or 1000 trees? Clearly huge numbers of insects (and other animals), representing many thousands of species, could be killed or forced to migrate to other trees. However, *losses of species* (rather than individuals) are difficult to predict until more is known about their abundance, their spatial distribution or geographic range, and their relationships to particular plant species.

If all insect species are uniformly distributed within a particular habitat and are able to live on any tree species then the 'direct proportion' assumption of Question 2.3 can be used to predict losses of individuals of particular species. This reduction in numbers of individuals may, in turn, lead to the demise of a given species (increasing its probability of extinction, Section 4.4.1). However, uniform spatial distribution and indifference to host plants is manifestly not the case for many insect species. Many herbivorous insect species are restricted to *one* tree species, perhaps feeding on, for example, just the seed of that tree species. Furthermore, certain parasitic insects (such as the Chalcidoidea mentioned above, most of which are egg, larval or pupal parasites) may feed *only* on that herbivorous insect species. If these specialist parasites lose their host insect, and the specialist herbivorous insects lose their host tree, then they will become extinct. The herbivorous insects may occupy only a small part of the geographic range of the tree and, likewise, the parasites may be limited to a small part of the range of the host insect. For example, consider the information shown in Figure 6.2; a particular tree species has a wide geographic distribution (grey area in Figure 6.2) but a specialist herbivorous insect feeding exclusively on that tree occurs only in a narrower geographic range (pale green area in Figure 6.2). A parasitic insect feeds only on this herbivorous species, but is found only within a restricted area (green area in Figure 6.2). The effect of deforestation will therefore depend on where the destruction occurs in relation to the distribution of species and on the interactions between species.

▷ What is the effect of deforestation in area A in Figure 6.2 compared with area B?

▶ In area A there would be no loss of the specialist herbivore or its parasitoid. In area B all parasitic insects would be lost together with some herbivorous insects. (The loss of the parasitic insects *might* have a net benefit for the remaining herbivorous insects.)

Unfortunately many of the details of plant–herbivore and herbivore–parasitoid relationships and ecology are unknown in the tropics, and so many key questions remain unanswered. Most of the information on, for example, the degree of specialization of

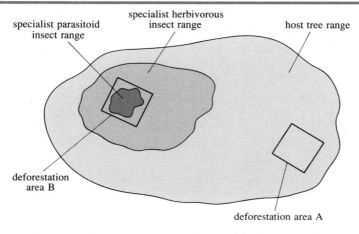

Figure 6.2 Hypothetical geographic ranges of a host tree species (the whole shaded area), a specialist insect herbivore (pale green) and its specialist parasitoid (green). The effects of deforestation in areas A and B are considered in the text.

parasitic insects, has come from temperate regions. This is yet another example where knowledge of the underlying science is essential for predicting the effects of habitat loss.

6.2.3 An alternative to the direct proportion assumption

The loss of species in direct proportion to habitat loss has been questioned several times in this book. An alternative to that assumption is described briefly in this section: a non-linear relationship between loss of species and habitats, in the form of **species–area curves**. These, as the name suggests, relate the number of species to a given area. Generally, they refer to the number of species of a particular taxonomic group, e.g. birds or reptiles or butterflies, but occasionally a number of such groups may be lumped together.

An example of such a relationship was found when the number of plant species was recorded from different sized nature reserves in Yorkshire. By plotting a series of measurements of number of species and reserve area it was possible to construct the curve shown in Figure 6.3.

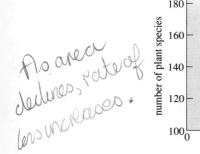

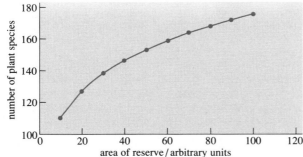

Figure 6.3 A species–area curve showing the relationship between the number of plant species in some Yorkshire nature reserves and the area of the reserves. Note that relationships of this type can generally be described by equations of the form $S = cA^b$, where S is the number of species in area A, and b and c are parameters, i.e. values held constant in a particular application of the equation. The values of b and c are estimated by plotting $\log_{10}$ (species) against $\log_{10}$ (area). If plants on a set of reserves from different geographical sites are compared (e.g. nature reserves in Yorkshire and Lancashire), values of b are likely to be similar between sites, and values of c are likely to be similar. However, they are likely to be different if plants are compared to birds. The parameter values in this example are c = 70 and b = 0.20, so that the equation of the curve is $S = 70A^{0.2}$.

We can use the graph in Figure 6.3 to illustrate the effect of decreasing the area by a fixed amount.

Question 6.1 With reference to Figure 6.3:

(a) (i) What is the effect on the number of plant species of reducing the area by 20 units from 100 to 80?

(ii) What is the effect on the number of plant species of reducing the area from 40 to 20 units?

(b) Given the results of (a), what is the important difference between the 'direct proportion' assumption for effects of habitat reduction and that derived from considerations of species–area curves?

The relationships described by species–area curves, therefore, allow predictions about the effect on species richness of reducing the area of a particular habitat by a given amount. These techniques have been applied to tropical moist forests and other habitats, and have produced *global* estimates of loss of total species of about 0.12% per year (assuming about one-half of all species live in tropical moist forests) over the next few years. Of course, from your answer to Question 6.1 you will be aware that this predicted rate of extinction would be likely to increase as the habitat area decreases.

▷ How many species will be lost each year given a total species count of 10 million?

▶ 0.12% of 10 million species = $0.12/100 \times (10 \times 10^6) = 1.2 \times 10^4$ species per year.

This estimate can then be compared with 28 500 per year in the tropical moist forests (or 57 000 world-wide) estimated by the direct proportion method (Question 2.3). Thus the two methods have given estimates of 12 000 (species–area) and 57 000 (direct proportion) for the annual loss of species. Whilst this is a large difference it is worth remembering that the rate of loss predicted by the species–area method will catch up with that of the direct proportion method as habitat destruction proceeds to remove more and more tropical moist forest.

6.2.4 The temperate parallel

Loss of biodiversity is not restricted to terrestrial systems nor to tropical areas. A good example of the loss of biodiversity has come from recent work on freshwater fish in temperate areas, which is summarized in Extract 6.3. As you read this extract, note that taxon (plural taxa) is a taxonomic unit, which can be species, genus, family, etc. (in this case, it is species), and biota means flora and fauna.

Extract 6.3   From P. B. Moyle and J. E. Williams (1990) *Conservation Biology*, **4**, pp. 275–284.

In proportion to the entire fauna, loss of species may be as great in temperate regions as in tropical regions. To test the validity of this statement we analyzed the status of the native fish fauna of California, using a methodology that quantifies expert knowledge. Of 113 native taxa, 6% are extinct, 12% are officially listed as threatened or endangered, 6% deserve immediate listing, 17% may need listing soon, 22% show declining populations but are not yet in serious trouble and 36% seem to be secure. Much of the faunal decline has taken place in recent years; it has included unexpectedly rapid declines of once abundant species. Fish taxa in serious trouble are likely to be (1) endemic to California [i.e. the species is found only in the area under consideration], (2) restricted to a small area, (3) occupants of just one drainage basin, (4) part of a fish assemblage of less than five species and (5) found in isolated springs, warm water streams or big rivers. Water diversions and introduced species, acting in concert, seem to be the principal causes of the decline of the native fauna, although other types of habitat degradation have contributed as well. The situation in California, with its high degree of endemism (60%), may be regarded as extreme but fish faunas in other temperate regions show signs of being nearly as stressed. It is likely that the situation with fish reflects a more general decline of the biota of temperate regions of the world.

Factors 1 and 2 (endemism, and restriction to a small area), which affect the chances of extinction of the fish fauna, relate directly to the points made in Figure 6.2 and Section 6.2.2. Endemic species occur nowhere else and, if also restricted to a small area within California, are highly susceptible to extinction due to, for example, localized habitat destruction or degradation. This emphasizes again the importance of knowing the geographical range of species when predicting the effects of habitat loss.

▷ Can you think of an example of the 'other types of habitat degradation' referred to in Extract 6.3?

▶ There are a number of possibilities, including pollution and drying-up of river beds.

6.3 Why save biological diversity?

Now we know what biological diversity is, why is it desirable to conserve it? If we stick rigidly to the definition of diversity given at the start of this chapter, then there are two related requirements to maintain a high diversity; (1) to conserve the maximum number of species and (2) to maintain species at similar levels. Generally, conservation of diversity is taken to be equivalent to the first requirement. It is not necessary to make all species equally abundant—this is ecological nonsense (consider equal numbers of ants and elephants!). Nevertheless, it is important to maintain a high number of individuals per species in order to minimize their probability of extinction (Section 4.4.1). Conserving world biological diversity can be seen as equivalent to maintaining the present numbers of species on Earth—a loss of a species contributes to loss of biological diversity. This need is being recognized amongst government and non-government organizations, and was exemplified by the biodiversity convention at the 1992 'Earth Summit' in Rio de Janeiro. For example, the British Government's Overseas Development Administration (ODA) published the booklet *Biological Diversity and Developing Countries* in 1991, which expresses both the desire to conserve biodiversity and the reasons why it is desirable:

> *Biodiversity refers to the variety and variability of all animals, plants and micro-organisms on Earth. Some of this diversity is essential, in that mankind is dependent on other species for the maintenance of the biosphere and the supply of basic necessities, particularly food. A larger proportion of biodiversity is considered valuable because of the goods and services provided by other species, and because of the potential inherent in what has been described as the world's most fundamental capital stock.*

This quotation focuses on the need to conserve the components of biodiversity (species, represented as 'goods and services'), both in terms of what are used now and what may be needed in the future, rather than diversity *per se*. In the former sense, conservation of biodiversity is equivalent to conservation for *resources* (Chapter 3).

▷ How does this compare with the reasons for conserving biodiversity presented in Extract 6.1?

▶ Very similar—Extract 6.1 emphasized the use of pharmaceutical products, i.e. that biodiversity constitutes a pool of resources for human use. You will recall that the medical uses of species and their potential commercial value were described in Extract 3.6.

But why is diversity *per se* desirable? The most often quoted reason is that ecological *diversity* and ecological *stability* are closely linked. In other words, if ecological diversity becomes too low then the ecological system becomes unstable, with the result that more species become extinct, contributing to lower diversity, and so on. In the most extreme scenario the system can become locked into a positive feedback loop of declining stability and diversity.

In considering these processes from a scientific point of view, it is necessary to be clear what is meant by the *stability* of an ecological system. There can be community stability *or* population stability *or* ecosystem stability.* In all cases, the concern is with the ability of the system to maintain itself at a steady state or *equilibrium*. In Section 4.4.1 equilibrium was discussed in the context of population size. Here the concept of equilibrium is considered in more general terms, in which stability can be defined in terms of perturbations away from the equilibrium (Figure 6.4). The idea of stability can be likened to a ball in a bowl. At the bottom of the bowl (A) the ball does not move. It therefore appears to be at equilibrium (a steady-state). This apparent stability can be investigated by pushing the ball in one direction and seeing what happens (Figure 6.4b). The displacement (or perturbation) test has therefore confirmed that position A is a stable equilibrium. The displacement or perturbation test is necessary because the ball may be sitting at an *un*stable equilibrium (Figures 6.4c and d).

Translating the theoretical ideas into ecological practice means equating position A to the relative abundances of species in an ecological community. The ball is then the community, i.e. the relative numbers of individuals of each species , and moving the ball is equivalent to altering the relative abundances of species in the community. A community with a single stable equilibrium will tend to return to the relative proportions of species at the stable equilibrium.

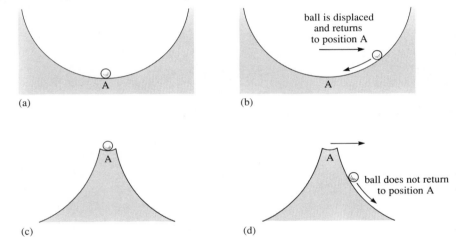

Figure 6.4 The concept of ecological stability. (a) A stable equilibrium, with (b) showing the result of displacing the ball, so that it returns to position A. (c) An unstable equilibrium, with (d) showing the result of displacing the ball, so that it does not return to A.

▷ How could a perturbation be applied to an ecological community to investigate its stability?

▶ By changing the relative abundance of the species, e.g. by reducing the number of individuals of one species.

Scientifically, the relationship between diversity and stability is far from clear. First, there is evidence from model systems that low diversity systems may be more stable than their complex, high diversity counterparts. Second, it appears that there are a large number of ecosystems in the world that are stable but that have a relatively low diversity. Even amongst the tropical forests, which are generally thought of as highly diverse, there are examples where only one or two tree species dominate. Joseph Connell and Margaret Lowman stated in a scientific paper in 1989 that in some tropical forests '50–100% by number of canopy trees are one species'. In the north-eastern basin of the Congo river, at least two-thirds of the area is occupied by rainforests dominated by a single species. Such examples reveal that stability is *not necessarily* linked to high species diversity.

---

* Ecosystem stability may refer to phenomena such as the maintenance of nutrient supplies or oxygen levels. These phenomena, whilst of great importance in biological conservation, are unfortunately outside the scope of this book.

So we are left with two contradicting theories about the relationship between species diversity and stability. On the one hand, it is possible that every species is important and that the loss of a single one will reduce the stability of the system. On the other hand, some species may not be essential and their loss will not reduce the stability of the system.

It may seem unsatisfactory to end on yet another indeterminate point. However, it is perhaps an appropriate parting thought in that it reminds us not only of the need for greater scientific understanding but also that the ecological systems within which biological conservation is undertaken are so complex that there may be few general or unifying principles.

Summary of Chapter 6

1   Species diversity of an ecological community can be quantified with respect to the evenness and richness of species composition.

2   Biodiversity is a popular term which is often taken to mean global species richness.

3   A large fraction of terrestrial species richness is represented by insects—of which a large proportion are to be found in tropical ecosystems. Intensive tree canopy sampling and related studies in the last two decades have begun to reveal the extent of insect species richness in the tropics.

4   Despite the studies of the last 20 years there remain very large gaps in knowledge of the distribution and abundance of insect species in tropical forests. This means that it is extremely difficult to predict the effects of deforestation in anything but crude theoretical terms.

5   The need for biological diversity goes beyond thinking of species as resources; the maintenance of a certain (unknown) number of species *may* be critical for ensuring ecosystem or community stability.

Activity 6.4   *You should spend up to 1 hour on this activity.*

(a) Draw a series of labelled boxes, joined by arrows, that together summarize the main content of Chapter 6. Do so by first identifying the essential concepts and questions that the chapter addresses. Identify no more than a dozen such phrases; you might include for example, biodiversity, Simpson diversity index, quantifying diversity in tropical forests, effects of deforestation, relationship between diversity and stability, etc. Now arrange your full set of phrases into an orderly and logical sequence of labelled boxes, joined where possible by arrows. Aim to produce a diagram that you could use to explain the key points of Chapter 6 to a fellow student.

Study the answer to (a) before you tackle (b) and (c) below.

(b) Now attempt the same exercise on the contents of each of Chapters 1–5. Construct one such diagram for Chapters 1 and 2; construct separate diagrams for the remaining chapters, in a consistent style. Adopt the same approach as in (a), and once again aim to produce diagrams that will remind you of key points. To avoid making the diagrams too complex use no more than about a dozen labelled boxes in each diagram.

(c) Chapter 6 is in some respects a culmination of ideas outlined earlier in the book, drawing together important strands. Use your diagrams in (b) to write down at least *two* topics from Chapters 1–5 that relate most clearly to the coverage of biodiversity in Chapter 6.

---

7 Where do we go from here?

In this book a wide range of conservation problems and solutions have been debated, and summarized at the end of the chapters and in Activity 6.4. It is therefore appropriate at this point to consider where we go from here. Given the current problems, and the responses of scientists and others, can we say how these responses are being, or could be, improved or developed?

It is unlikely that the suite of scientific responses discussed in Chapters 4, 5 and 6 will be fundamentally altered. One will always need good monitoring information, there will always be a need for effective management (coupled with protection), and there is an increasing need to consider the whole ecological system, i.e. species, habitats, chemical and physical factors. Any developments are therefore likely to come within this framework.

In terms of monitoring there is a need for more effective methods of gathering, processing and distributing data on endangered species and habitats. This need is being met by the increased use of computerized databases linked to other software such as Geographical Information Systems (GIS). With this type of software it is possible to keep records of the geographic range of species, population size, habitat preferences, and threats to species. Imagine a situation where such software is used to establish the likelihood of a species becoming extinct. Information on range, population size, etc., can be combined to produce probabilities of extinction, which can be displayed in map form, perhaps indicating areas of highest risk. Effective databases of species distribution and population size can help the data-gathering process by identifying geographical areas or species where little information is available.

Effective management of species and habitats, as seen in Chapter 5, depends on a detailed knowledge of the response of species to particular habitat changes. Field experiments, in which habitat factors are manipulated in a systematic way, are becoming increasingly popular. For example, how does increasing the amount of food available to a population influence the size and dynamics of the population? Such experiments allow one to pinpoint more precisely the exact factors that determine the survival and fecundity of individuals in a particular place. As with monitoring, the incorporation of such information into Expert Systems—software which produces suggestions for management (or any other application) based on existing knowledge and local field conditions—can improve the rate of transfer of knowledge from scientists to practitioners.

The biodiversity discussion in Chapter 6 highlighted the need for increased information on, for example, tropical forest canopy insects. These needs would be met by some of the developments considered under monitoring, along with increased financial resources! Chapter 6 also hinted at a greater requirement for understanding the processes that determine species diversity, so that the consequences of habitat reduction or degradation can be predicted more accurately. These processes would include considerations of species–area and stability–diversity relationships. In fact, these are areas of study which have been worked on by ecologists for many years. Given the amount of work already undertaken, it is not clear whether even greatly accelerated activity in this area would take us forward at a fast enough rate. There is a good chance that by the time the workings of tropical forests, for example, are fully understood, there will be virtually none of them left!

In this book, we have only been able to consider a few of the ways in which biological conservation is developing.

Clearly some avenues of development are going to be more fruitful than others. It would seem that it is the more basic, practical measures such as increased management efficiency, as opposed to more esoteric areas such as stability–diversity relationships, that are ultimately going to make the difference between plant or animal species remaining extant or becoming extinct. Whatever the future developments in this important topic, if you now feel better equipped to follow those developments, then this book will have achieved its purpose.

Further reading

Barbier, E. B., Burgess, J. C., Swanson, T. M. and Pearce, D. W. (1990) *Elephants, Economics and Ivory*, Earthscan Publications.
Provides a detailed account of the economics of the ivory trade; useful data but written from a particular perspective.

Collins, M. (ed.) (1990) *The Last Rainforests*, IUCN and Mitchell Beazley.
Based on the IUCN database; good maps of threatened, lost and existing forest with details of how forests work.

Fiedler, P. and Jain, S. K. (eds) (1992) *Conservation Biology*, Chapman and Hall.
A collection of articles by researchers, so technical but readable.

Goldsmith, F. B. (ed.) (1991) *Monitoring for Conservation and Ecology*, Chapman and Hall.
A useful summary of methods of monitoring based on a series of articles by researchers.

Gradwohl, J. and Greenberg, R. (1988) *Saving the Tropical Forests*, Earthscan Publications.
Popular text with a large number of well described case studies.

Usher, M. B. (1973) *Biological Management and Conservation*, Chapman and Hall.
Out-of-date and quite technical, but an important text book with a large number of insights into scientific management and other aspects of conservation biology.

Skills

In this section we list skills that have been explicitly taught and/or revised in this book. You should find that most of them are special instances of the general skills categories given in the *Course Study Guide*, although some of them (5, 6 and 7) are rooted in the particular content of this book.

1   Interpret and manipulate data presented in the form of text, tables, graphs, diagrams and maps. (*Questions 2.2, 3.1, 3.3, 4.1–4.7 and 6.1; Activities 2.1, 4.1 and 4.3*)

2   Convert data between different mathematical, tabular and graphical forms and, where appropriate, compare the merits of different forms of presentation. (*Activities 4.1 and 6.3*)

3   Extract from an article, parts of which you may find unintelligible, information that is relevant to a particular question and, by integrating that information with what you already know, give an answer to the question in your own words. (*Question 5.1; Activities 3.1–3.4, 4.2, 5.1, 6.1 and 6.2*)

4   Summarize, in writing or using a flow chart, the main points from a section of text that you have studied. (*Activities 3.1, 3.4, 6.2 and 6.4*)

5   Identify and classify the nature of conservation problems. (*Question 4.9; Activity 1.1*)

6   Understand the methods used to obtain and estimate data on population size and species diversity and recognize associated limitations and assumptions. (*Questions 2.3, 2.5, 3.2, 4.4–4.6 and 6.1; Activities 4.2, 4.4 and 6.3*)

7   Appreciate the nature, importance and limitations of mathematical models that simulate population dynamics. (*Questions 4.7 and 4.8; Activities 4.3 and 4.4*)

8   Use information obtained from one source to comment on views expressed in another. (*Activities 3.2 and 6.1*)

9   Consider social, political and ethical aspects of a scientific issue. (*Activities 1.1, 3.1, 3.2 and 3.4*)

10 Formulate a personal opinion or strategy on a scientific issue. (*Activities 3.2 and 3.5*)

Answers to questions

Question 2.1

Common name	Genus	Species
human	*Homo*	*sapiens*
lady's slipper orchid	*Cypripedium*	*calceolus*

Question 2.2

(a) The vertical scale is inverted, with the lowest temperature at the top and the highest at the bottom.

(b) The increase in precipitation at a temperature of 25 °C results in vegetation changing from grassland, through tropical seasonal forest to tropical rainforest.

Question 2.3

Using the estimate of 1.8 million species, half of which are in tropical forests, (see the beginning of Section 2.2.1), gives a value of 0.9 million species in tropical forests. The estimated rate of forest loss is 0.57% per year (Activity 2.1a), so the estimated loss of species is

$$= 0.9 \times 10^6 \times \frac{0.57}{100} \text{ per year}$$

$$= 5130 \text{ per year}$$

$$\approx 14 \text{ per day.}$$

Using the estimate of 10 million predicted species world-wide, and therefore of 5 million in the forest, the loss is

$$= 5 \times 10^6 \times \frac{0.57}{100} \text{ per year}$$

$$= 28500 \text{ per year}$$

$$\approx 78 \text{ per day.}$$

Question 2.4

The missing words are species, habitat, population.

Question 2.5

The problems encountered were mentioned in Section 2.2.1, in the context of tropical moist forests. A major problem is the accurate knowledge of the number of species present *before* loss of any habitat. Then establishing whether a particular species becomes extinct or not is clearly a difficult and time-consuming process! A second major difficulty is obtaining accurate information on the *rate* of habitat loss.

You may have thought of additional complications—for example, it is uncertain whether species loss is proportional to habitat loss and the extinction of species can obviously occur for reasons other than habitat loss, e.g. hunting, and the introduction of new, 'alien' species. Note too that 'exploitation' of habitats (e.g. by logging) can reduce numbers of species without the full loss of the habitat.

Question 2.6

The example given in Section 2.3.2 was *grazing* by sheep or by rabbits. Grassland is maintained by this process because the course of natural succession is slowed down as, for example, some young trees and shrubs are selectively eaten (also see Section 2.1.2). The processes of management and of natural succession in grassland will be looked at in more detail in Chapter 5.

Question 3.1

There was a sharp drop in the numbers of all whales caught from 1939 to 1945, i.e. during World War II.

Except for the war years, the number of blue whales caught dropped fairly steadily from 30 000 in 1930 to about 2 000 in the late 1950s.

The numbers of fin whales caught rose rapidly in the 1930s and, except for the war years, remained high (>20 000) through to the late 1950s.

Question 3.2

That harvesting efforts remained constant during the period of study. In fact, apart from the war years, harvesting effort increased, suggesting that the reduction in numbers was even more dramatic than that shown in Figure 3.1.

Question 3.3

The total reduction of approximately 586 000 in Table 3.4 is halfway between the predicted totals of 402 305–796 050 over the period 1979–1987 (Table 3.3), suggesting that much of the reduction in elephant numbers during the 1980s can be accounted for by culling for ivory.

Question 4.1

The range of the early spider orchid in Britain has contracted towards the south-east. Before 1930, the species was present over much of central and southern England, up to an imaginary line joining the Severn and the Wash. By 1975, only a few locations on the south coast and in south-east England remained. (In fact, the number of 10 km × 10 km squares containing the early spider orchid fell from 47 in 1930 to 10 in 1975.)

Question 4.2

Numbers are fairly constant at about 80 plants in the 20 m × 20 m plot during 1975–1978 and 1983–1984. Between 1978 and 1983 a drop in the population occurred, reaching a minimum of about 10 plants in 1980.

Question 4.3

The fact that individuals may remain dormant underground for five years suggests that this is the minimum time over which a project on survival should be run. In other words, finishing the project after, for example, 3 years would lead to individuals being recorded as dead when they were in fact dormant. It may, of course, be that individuals could survive dormant for longer than 5 years: however, the shape of the histogram in Figure 4.3 suggests that these occurrences would be extremely rare.

Question 4.4

(a) From Equation 4.1, $N = D/(R \times A)$

Therefore the estimated number of elephants in the park, $N = \dfrac{8\,267\,000}{17 \times 188} = 2\,587.$

(b) All are estimates for various reasons; they are all average values based on sets of data collected under particular conditions. D is given as an estimate as it is an average value based on counts in relatively small areas, e.g. $100\,\text{m} \times 100\,\text{m}$. R is an average across different ages of elephant, collected either from field observations or from elephants in zoos. A is also an average value; the values of A will vary dependent upon the place where the dung is dropped and the activities of decomposers.

(c) This could be checked either by using another sampling technique, e.g. by aeroplane (Extract 3.1), or by repeating sampling over several years.

Question 4.5

(a) From Equation 4.2, $T = \dfrac{N_1 \times N_2}{M_2} = \dfrac{48 \times 100}{15} = 320$.

(b) It is also assumed that the animals mix back into the population evenly after marking.

Question 4.6

The mean population sizes are 2 186 for the chalkhill blue and 345 for the marbled white.

Question 4.7

The multiplication rate is the number of eggs in year $t + 1$ (250), divided by the number in year t (100) = 250/100 = 2.5. By year 3, there will be $250 \times 2.5 = 625$, and by year 4, $625 \times 2.5 = 1\,562.5$.

Question 4.8

The results would not be exactly the same because they are dependent upon the roll of a die. However, if the number of trials for a given initial population size are sufficiently high a *similar* answer would be expected for the probability of extinction. For example, if you and I had both started with a population size of 5, you might have got 65 out of 100 extinctions within 20 years, whilst I might have achieved 61 out of 100.

Question 4.9

The categories are more explicit with less overlap than the IUCN categories. They also incorporate data on population size and distribution, as described in the present chapter. For example, natural rarity and the distribution of populations, which includes their relative isolation, are included in the ****, *** and ** categories. The categories also incorporate information on animals in programmes of captive breeding or other controlled conditions.

Question 5.1

(a) Domestic stock, e.g. cattle or sheep, may also be used to graze chalk grassland. They would have the advantage of being easier to control than rabbits, and have greater economic benefits to land-owners.

(b) *Juniperus* (juniper), and *Crataegus monogyna* (hawthorn) increased.

(c) Ragwort (*Senecio jacobaea*) and other poisonous plants such as *Atropa belladonna* (deadly nightshade) and *Cynoglossum officinale* (hound's-tongue) decreased. When rabbits were abundant, these poisonous plants were avoided, and rabbits consumed their competitors. In addition, certainly for ragwort, the rabbits created suitable conditions for seed germination. After the decline of the rabbits, these germination sites and space for adult plants were no longer available in such a large quantity due to invasion by coarse grasses and, subsequently, woody species.

Question 6.1

(a) (i) The number of species at 100 area units is just below 180; at 80 it is about 170, so the reduction in the number of species is about 10 (the reduction calculated from the equation is in fact 7.7).

(ii) The number of species at 40 area units is about 150; at 20 it is 130, so the reduction in the number of species is about 20.

(b) As the area declines, so the *rate* of loss of species *increases*. This compares with the 'direct proportion' assumption where the rate of species loss is assumed to be constant.

Answers to activities

Activity 1.1

(a)   It is likely that all the problems stem directly or indirectly from human influences, with the possible exception of 2 and 10.

The evidence is strongest in 1 (agricultural pressures), 3 (pollution), 4 and 9 (fire), 5 and 8 (hunting), 6 (accident) and 7 (fishing).

These extracts can offer only a fragment of each story and you may be tempted to speculate on the underlying causes. The reason for the fall in sea-bird populations (2) is uncertain, but over-fishing by humans may be a contributory factor. Pollution and loss of freshwater habitats probably contribute to loss of fish species in 10, though this is unlikely to be the whole explanation. The fall in kakapo numbers (6) is known to be linked to habitat loss and to the predation of this defenceless bird by introduced species.

(b)   The clearest example of direct exploitation is by hunting, 5 and 8. Both the orang-utan and the rhinoceros are used (illegally) as a biological 'resource', which accounts for their diminished numbers. You will learn more about both examples later in the book.

(c)   As Extract 4 implies, the leisure activities of humans can be in conflict with the requirements of biological conservation. Sometimes the influence of humans is accidental and indirect.

(d)   The clearest examples are 1 and 3. As mentioned in the answer to question (a) 2, 6 and 10 *may* be linked with loss of habitat or with over-exploitation, both attributable largely or wholly to human activities. It is now well established that golden lion tamarins are vulnerable largely as a consequence of habitat destruction so 9 is also a candidate.

(e)   The most obvious strategies are the breeding of endangered species in zoos (1), and the re-introduction of species into habitats from which they have been lost (7). Less obvious, though equally important, is the restoration of degraded habitats (9).

Protection of breeding species is clearly a priority (3). Extract 8 describes captive breeding for commercial purposes, which is arguably of benefit to wild populations. Although you will not know this from the extract, the success described in 6 is also the result of a breeding programme, aimed at increasing numbers of the kakapo. (The same breeding programme is mentioned in Extract 6 of Figure 1.1.)

(f)   (i) 8, (ii) 10. The relationship between commercial interests and conservation strategies will be considered in later chapters.

(g)   5; here habitat conservation is seen as sufficiently important to warrant eradication of a threatening species. But the policy touches on broader issues and the type of conflict of interest mentioned in (f).

(h)   A case could be made for a need for more information for *any* of the items in Figure 1.2—as this the book will show, sound conservation practice has to build on 'good' science. Extracts 2 and 4 are especially good examples of this general principle. The former is driven by the need to find out whether numbers of marine mammals are declining and if so, is it as a result of pollutants? The latter example shows that an essential first step in conservation is to locate and count threatened species, taking advantage of local knowledge!

Activity 2.1

(a)   The average annual deforestation rate for 1976–1980 was 6113×10^3 ha per year. If this is divided by the global total of forest existing in 1980 then we can find the average percentage loss per year:

$$\frac{6113 \times 10^3}{1081372 \times 10^3} \times 100 = 0.57\%.$$

(b)   Either consider *absolute* values for deforestation in terms of hectares lost per year (see column 3 of Table 2.2), or loss of forest *relative* to the estimate of the total amount of forest existing in 1980 (column 2 of Table 2.2). This would involve expressing the values in column 3 as a percentage of the values in the middle column, as you did for the totals in (a).

(c)   With the first approach, Brazil, Colombia, Indonesia, Ecuador and Malaysia top the list. With the second method, the top five are Ecuador, (2.1%) Colombia (1.7%), Madagascar (1.6%), Malaysia (1.1%) and Mexico (1.1%). (*Note*: Short-cuts can be useful in an exercise of this type! You do not need to calculate the percentage for *each* row in Table 2.2. You could first scan the numbers to try to identify the countries with high deforestation rates (column 3) but small areas of forest (column 2), before calculating the percentage to verify your observations.)

(d)   The general message here is a familiar one—manipulation of data can change the message conveyed! The second arithmetical approach might be used to disguise the fact that Brazil and Indonesia undertook major programmes of deforestation in the late 1970s, but because their remaining forested areas are so vast the *relative* rates of loss are *lower* than some other countries (e.g. Mexico) whose deforestation programmes are less in the public eye. Finally, bear in mind that the data in Table 2.2 refer to the late 1970s—it is certain that current rates of deforestation would differ from Table 2.2 in a number of respects.

Activity 3.1

(a)

For a relaxation of the ban:

Scientific	Economic	Others
Elephant populations 'thriving'.	Support conservation by ploughing back profits from ivory.	Culls are required at present.
Destruction of habitat.	Present ivory stockpile cannot be sold.	Need to retain Zimbabwe and other African states within CITES.
	Increased requirement for land.	
	Trading would prompt local communities to protect parks and elephants.	
	Insufficient aid available to support alternative forms of conservation.	

Against a relaxation of the ban:

Scientific	Economic	Others
Uncertain accuracy of population counts/ no knowledge of ability of populations to recover.	Relaxation of ban 'too risky'—black market prices soared at hint of relaxation.	Fear of revival of pre-1989 poaching epidemic.
Difficulty of verification, i.e. distinguishing between legal and illegal ivory.	Tourism the key to saving African mammals.	'Thin end of the wedge argument', e.g. effect on leopard skin and rhino horn trade.

You may have thought of additional factors or have expressed these points differently, but I hope your answer reveals that the case for a relaxation of the ban depends more on economic considerations than on scientific issues!

(b)   Writing a letter of this type requires clear advocacy of a point of view using the points that support the case for opposing relaxation of the ban. Remember the need to focus on the *scientific* case so not all of the points identified in (a) against a relaxation of the ban will be relevant. My attempt is as follows:

> *To the Editor,*
>
> *The scientific reasoning behind what has been termed by the Environmental Investigation Agency 'the largest state-sanctioned kill of elephants in history' is unconvincing. Zimbabwe's wildlife scientists claim that their elephant populations are booming and that culls are therefore essential, opening the way to use of the ivory stockpile so generated. But it is doubtful if their wildlife park populations of elephants could have increased as fast as claimed—more likely this reflects the uncertainties of conducting an elephant census. The scope for error is high, in part because of our ignorance of the elephants' migratory habits. Thus, an unknown proportion of the estimated 68 000 Zimbabwe elephants may be immigrants from neighbouring countries, perhaps drawn in to the habitat vacated by earlier culls.*
>
> *Surely, the recent ominous increase in the black market value of ivory, when rumours of a restoration of ivory trading emerged, is evidence enough of the dire consequences of adopting the proposals for relaxation of the ban. There is as yet no scientifically proven method of distinguishing ivory from different sources, so passing illegal ivory as legal—common practice prior to the 1989 ban on ivory trading—would bedevil any attempt at regulating harvesting. Indeed, any move towards a restoration of trading, for the possible benefit of a few African countries, is surely too risky a strategy in view of the increasingly difficult future faced by the African elephant.*
>
> *Yours sincerely etc.*

Read through your own letter and spend some time reflecting on its content. You may have brought in additional points, for example the low rates of population growth in elephants. In what sense is your draft better/worse than my own efforts given above?

Activity 3.2

The answer to both (a) and (b) has to be your own. Nevertheless, you might find it useful to consider my attitude, though it claims to be no more right than yours.

(a)   I do not support any relaxation of the ban. The economic interests of a few African nations should take second place to the continent-wide conservation of the species. Restoration of ivory trading would surely lead to a dramatic increase in ivory poaching.

I find it difficult to condemn the *principle* of conservation through sustainable utilization, which may prove a necessary and effective strategy for preservation of plant and animal species. However, there are clear problems of implementation, as we have seen. In my view, culling and ivory trading should be regarded as separate issues—a policy followed by the Kenyan government.

(b)   My attitude is (I would claim) primarily based on scientific rationality. Of uppermost concern in my mind is the difficulty of verification, of accurately estimating the size of elephant populations and the low population growth rate of the elephant. Thus the margin for error in a policy of sustainable harvesting is very small (and, in part, unknown). This coupled with my cynical view of human nature, especially when a lot of money is at stake, suggests that any policy of regulated trade will be subject to abuse. It is therefore difficult for me to claim that scientific logic is the *only* reason for my view on the relationship between commerce and conservation—here feelings about my fellow humans are to the fore.

Activity 3.3

(a)

o Moved desert black rhinos have difficulty with feeding (gut bacteria).

o Moved desert black rhinos have difficulties establishing new territory.

o Desert black rhinos are moved to an unusual habitat. Desert rhinos are opportunistic feeders, e.g. they will eat grass which is quite different from the diet of normal black rhino (browsers, mainly leaves).

(b) Precautions are required during and after the application of the anaesthetic, and checks are needed to ensure that there are no long-term deleterious effects.

o Avoid stimulatory effects of M99 by mixing with sedative.

o Apply respiratory stimulant to maintain breathing.

o Prevent overheating—throw water over the rhino during exposure.

o Antiseptic applied to stump to avoid infection from abrasion.

o Check that absence of horn does not affect social interactions, e.g. feeding, fighting, reproductive appeal.

(c) (i) Work on diet of desert black rhino reveals why translocation to novel habitats is not appropriate.

(ii) Susceptibility to raised body temperature and response to drugs reveals importance of cooling animal and avoidance of a prolonged chase.

Activity 3.4

(a) Fellows blames the fact that change 'has not been economically viable nor politically expedient'. This strikes me as an admirably succinct and accurate explanation of the lack of significant progress since the 1972 Stockholm conference.

(b) Section 3.3 talks in terms of 'biological resources', which come under Fellows' 'direct use' category. Fellows' categorization reminds us that the economic value of plants goes beyond this—both in terms of the aesthetic (i.e. non-use value, see Section 3.1), and *indirect* and *optional* use values. We will return to the indirect use value in Chapter 6.

(c) (i) Section 2.2.1 states that 'about one-half of all known species are found in the tropical rainforest'. This compares well with Fellows' estimate of the number of *plant* species in tropical moist forests as 'more than half of known plant species' with '60%' in all tropical forest types. (ii) Fellows reports a loss of all tropical forest of 7–8 million km^2 over the past 50 years or so. This represents an average *annual* rate of loss of about 150 000 km^2 or 15 million hectares. Table 2.2 gives a global loss of over 6 million hectares per year, based on figures for 1976–80. The implication is that there must have been much higher rates of deforestation in other periods to raise the average to 15 million. This sort of discrepancy is by no means uncommon in the literature and without the raw data we should be extremely cautious when making such comparisons. The other estimate that Fellows gives of annual *current* loss of rainforest is about 75 000 km^2 or 7.5 million hectares, which compares reasonably well with Table 2.2.

(d)   Fellows assumes here the continuation of 'present trends', which ignores the possibilities of (i) reductions in future population growth, (ii) improved efficiency in the future for 'marginal' farming, for example, crops genetically engineered to withstand drought better. However, even an 'optimistic' view of the future predicts a sharp increase in deaths from famine in Africa in the next century.

(e)   Principe has estimated the 'foregone market value' of those drugs with a reasonable likelihood of discovery, if species loss had been avoided. To derive this value, he (i) estimated the current average economic contribution per useful phytochemical (a little less than $390 million), (ii) the likelihood of any given plant yielding a marketable prescription drug (1 in 2 000), and (iii) the proportion of plant species lost by 2050 (25%). Principe's figures suggest that the present value of this foregone benefit is between $3.5 billion (using retail sales estimates alone) and $7 000 billion (including the economic value of saved lives). The lower value indicates the expenditure that should now be undertaken to safeguard against this future loss of benefits.

Summarizing a complex argument such as this is far from easy, but it is an important skill that you should become increasingly adept at as your study progresses.

(f)   With the 60-second 'advertisement', a balance has to be struck between factual content and dramatic presentation: in this activity we inevitably focus on the words and the presentation of facts. Fellow's argument will have to be presented in a simplified form.

My suggestion is to start by quoting figures for the rate of deforestation and the rate of population growth, which are stark and depressing. Then extract the simple 'take home message' from Principe's estimates, something like '… we are losing over 1 000 plant species per year. Doctors tell us that about 1 in every 2 000 plant species yields an important drug, vital in the fight against cancer and other diseases. So, the chances are that in every 2 years, one of the 2 000 plant species lost would have yielded a useful drug. Today's estimate is that each such species is worth about $400 million (note that this value has been rounded up to simplify the calculations), and that is just the loss in commercial terms. In terms of future deaths avoided and relief from suffering, the benefits are immeasurable, but all these drugs, along with the plants that produce them, are lost forever. And yet we still destroy the forest.' The 60 seconds could finish with a re-statement of the rates of deforestation.

Activity 3.5

These are, of course, difficult questions to address, but are important in that they reveal how far it is human choice and personal ethical codes that determine which species will ultimately survive. I can only give my own simplistic and personal reactions to each 'extreme' view.

Those of you at the 'no animals killed' end of the spectrum should consider the irony of residents of the 'developed' world telling people in tropical countries that they must not cut down the forest, when our own ancestors removed most of our own forests. Our concern is that we might lose species which might be useful for medicines or knowledge or which are aesthetically appealing. Clearly it is difficult to convince a poor farmer in a tropical country with this line of argument! Frequently, money made from, for example, pharmaceutical products has gone into the pockets of those in developed countries and not to those where the resource was harvested (but see the Fellows article). Non-use values need to be attached to species, such as tourists viewing elephants, which do not harm the animals themselves but also provide income to local people and developing world governments. This is a difficult formula to achieve, but certainly worth pursuing.

Those individuals at the 'any use' end of the spectrum may, of course, not care if species become extinct! But if you agree that preservation of species is desirable, the quandary faced is that of the legislators concerned with the ivory trade. Is it possible to have a *regulated* trade in ivory? There are two problems: one is determining exactly how much ivory can be removed without reducing the populations. This is essentially a scientific question and one which has received much attention from conservation biologists. The second problem is policing the trade. The black rhino example (Table 3.5) shows how difficult this can be. The amount of money required for effective policing may be far in excess of that fraction, generated by a regulated trade, which is returned to conservation. This is particularly true for large-bodied animals with a slow population growth rate. These populations can yield only very low amounts of resource without reducing the population size. The problem is therefore that extra money, from outside of the trade, may be needed to maintain a trade which is of benefit to few people.

Activity 4.1

(a)   You could plot (i) chalkhill blue numbers (vertical axis) against time (horizontal axis), (ii) marbled white numbers against time, or (iii) chalkhill blue numbers against marbled white numbers (it does not matter which way round these last two variables are plotted).

(b)   The trends (if present) that you would hope to reveal are changes with time in the numbers of chalkhill blue (i) or marbled white butterflies (ii), and whether the relative sizes of marbled white and chalkhill blue populations are related in any way (iii).

(c)   Figure 4.9 shows the three graphs. As graph (ii) indicates, the marbled white population increased in size over the first 9 years of sampling until 1986 and then declined in 1987. This pattern is similar to that for the chalkhill blue from 1981 to 1987 (i). Prior to 1981 the chalkhill blue had peaked and then declined in numbers. The fact that there is some similarity in the trends with time for the two species is borne out by graph (iii) which shows an overall positive relationship, i.e. both species

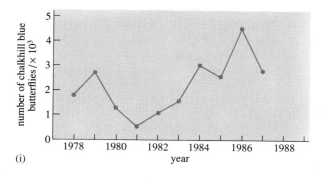

(i)

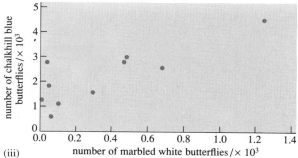

(iii)

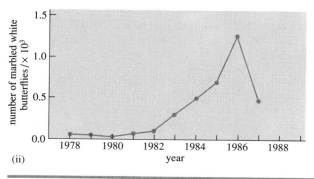

(ii)

Figure 4.9   Answer to Activity 4.1c. (i) Number of chalkhill blue butterflies plotted against time. (ii) Number of marbled white butterflies plotted against time. (iii) Number of chalkhill blue butterflies plotted against the number of marbled white butterflies.

have relatively high numbers in one year or relatively low numbers in one year. The scatter at lower values of the marbled white occurs because of the discrepancy in trends during 1978 to 1980.

Activity 4.2

(a)   The early references made in the paper (for example, to the work of Davenport, 1967) make it clear that orang-utans have long been known by conservationists to be resident in this area. (Note too, from the reference list at the end of the paper, that the author has helped conduct an earlier faunal survey in Sabah on large mammals—familiarity with the location is obviously a great help for conservationists seeking more information on a threatened species.)

(b)   (i) The main hindrance is that the animals occur usually in small groups and are shy and difficult to identify amongst the vegetation. (ii) Noisy calls and disturbances of the vegetation help locate orang-utan. Footprints and nest platforms also reveal their presence.

(c)   Walk-and-count listening (and looking) for individuals 40 m either side of the walker (i.e. the 80-m wide transect referred to in the text). Alternatively, an indirect sampling technique could be used, for example by counting nest platforms or droppings.

(d)   Here the author is noting the difficulty of extrapolating a value for mean population density for the entire area on the basis of only 20 sites. Remember that the objective of the sampling is to estimate the true population size in the area (and therefore estimate the density). The greater the number of sampling sites, the more likely it is that the mean population density estimated from the sampling is the same as the true (but unknown) mean population density. For a given number of sample sites it is possible to quantify the variation around the sample mean using the sample standard deviation, i.e. the spread of individual estimates from the 20 sites around the sample mean. The larger the sample standard deviation, the less certain we can be about determining the true mean population size. It may be that the author was referring to this type of calculation when he considered that too few data were collected.

(e)   The author does not say precisely how this population estimate was derived but the inference is that a mean population density is calculated and then multiplied by 5 000 km^2 (the primary forest area of eastern Sabah). If so, working backwards, the calculated mean population density would be 0.8 animals km^{-2}.

(f)   Rather few firm conclusions can be drawn as the data are so fragmentary! The design of the survey is sound (comparing matched sites of similar altitude) but the results are far from conclusive. For example, in Bakapit (a logged area) there were no orang-utan in 1980/81. However, the matched unlogged site (Tabin) also had a low ('present but rare') density of animals. Similarly, it is difficult to compare the data between the logged Malabuk site and the unlogged Kawag site (both at 220 m altitude) because the population densities at Malabuk are unknown. Unfortunately, there are no data for logged lowland forest to compare with Gomantong or Lungmanis where there are high (about 4 km^{-2}) population densities. Inconclusive data of this type very often emerge from the 'real world' of conservation, mainly because of the inherent difficulties of field studies.

(g)   The principal recommendation is that legal protection for orang-utans be provided in other areas of primary forest (notably the Danum valley). Interestingly, no firm recommendations are made with regard to loss of animals by hunting or through agricultural development, which looks set to become more prevalent in those parts of Sabah (the eastern lowlands) where orang-utans occur at their greatest density.

(h)   A central question relates to management of the forests—how might the commercial practice of logging be combined with effective conservation? In particular, to what extent can logged areas support viable numbers of orang-utan? Can the preservation of small unlogged areas of primary forest act as 'safe havens' for populations prior to their recolonization of regenerating logged areas?

Activity 4.3

(a)   See Figure 4.10a. To plot the graph of, for example, the multiplication rate of 2, first plot 10 on the vertical axis against 1 on the horizontal axis. Then at time (year) 2 the population has increased to $2 \times 10 = 20$, so plot 20 on the vertical axis against 2 on the horizontal axis, and so on.

(b)   The population with a multiplication rate of 2 doubles in size each year, the population with a multiplication rate of 1 remains constant in size with time whilst the population with a multiplication rate of 0.5 declines in size with time.

(c)   A population must have a multiplication rate equal to or greater than 1 to avoid extinction.

(d)   The multiplication rate of 2 is unrealistic over longer periods of time, because the population will reach an enormous size. This multiplication rate may, however, be realistic in the short term, e.g. over a few years.

(e)   See Figure 4.10b. To plot the graph with, for example, a multiplication rate of 2, proceed as for (a) except that the $\log_{10}$ of each population size is calculated. So, instead of plotting 10, 20, 40 and 80 against 1, 2, 3 and 4, you plot $\log_{10}(10) = 1$ against 1, $\log_{10}(20) = 1.30$ against 2 and so on. The advantage of the logarithmic plot is that the rate of change in population size over time is represented by the gradient of a straight line.

Figure 4.10   (a) Answer to Activity 4.3a, showing the change in population size over 4 years at three multiplication rates (mr). (b) Answer to Activity 4.3e, showing the change in the $\log_{10}$ (population size), at the same multiplication rates as in (a).

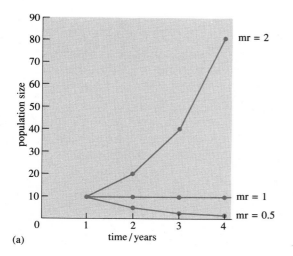

(a)

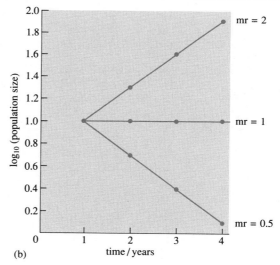

(b)

Activity 4.4

(a)   The first problem is to capture an orang-utan! To get the best estimate of population size one needs as many captured and marked animals as possible. The animals are large and tree-living, and to capture them requires a tranquillizer dart fired from a gun. You will recall from Extract 3.4 the problems of capturing a rhino for dehorning—with all the associated physiological difficulties. Assuming the orang-utan has been hit with the dart, then it needs to be caught as it drops from the tree! One of the assumptions of the mark–release–recapture method is that it does not affect the behaviour and survival of the animal—a drop of 40 m at a weight of up to 100 kg might not satisfy this assumption!

If one was able to capture sufficient numbers of animals, the next problem is to mark them. There are a variety of ways of marking animals, using ear tags or clipping fur or nails, but you would have to be certain that the method employed did not irritate the animal. The final problem (before trying to catch them again) is to release the animals back into their habitat. This might be a problem if the animals are young. The assumption of the mark–release–recapture method as an estimate of population size is that the marked animals mix back evenly into the population, but this may be a non-starter for an animal such as the orang-utan, which might be highly territorial, staying in a fixed area. Recaptures may tell you about the territorial range of the animal but nothing directly about population size. Indirectly, if something is known about the size of a territory, the population size can be guessed at, given the total area of suitable habitat.

Based on this discussion you would probably conclude that mark–release–recapture is an unsuitable method of population size estimation for large arboreal (tree-dwelling) animals.

(b)   For a model similar to that in Section 4.4.1, information on age-specific fecundity and survival is needed. Thus the number of offspring produced per female (of a given age) per year would be required together with the fraction of individuals surviving to a particular age under certain habitat conditions (e.g. logged vs. unlogged). Although the construction of the model would be more complicated than in Section 4.4.1, the result under density-independent conditions would be the same, i.e. the population would have a certain (fixed) multiplication rate. As with the butterfly model, the orang-utan model could be made more realistic by incorporating density-dependent factors (e.g. the density-dependent reduction in fecundity caused by increased immigration referred to in Extract 4.1) and variations in fecundity and survival.

Activity 5.1

(a)   The alternative land use is the planting of conifers. This would be an alternative method of generating income for upland estates, but would result in the loss of the flora and fauna currently associated with grouse moors.

(b)   The moorland is occasionally burnt to provide a moorland habitat with a *mosaic* including young heather (as fresh growth on burnt areas), which is the favoured food for grouse, and established heather, which provides cover for the birds. (Recall that the ideal chalk grassland habitat was a *mosaic* of long and short grass, Section 5.2.2.)

(c)   The ITE group believe that changes in the territorial behaviour of birds cause the cycles in population size. When numbers are high, birds leave fewer offspring (because of the eviction of many birds by other aggressive males). In contrast, the GC group believes that the cyclic fluctuations are produced by a parasitic worm (i.e. a helminth) that causes a debilitating and potentially lethal disease (after a time-lag) in these birds (this is implied in the extract—'reducing recruitment to the population through its effect on chick survival').

(d)   Little evidence is provided in the extract for the ITE interpretation but you could mention here (i) results showing that the relative aggressiveness of the birds' changes, and (ii) alterations in the inherited tolerance of birds depending on population density. The 'delay' mechanism at work is hinted at rather vaguely (changes in territory size). There is more emphasis on the GC theory, where you could quote (i) the fact that worm and grouse numbers vary in step, (ii) the relationship between the extent of cyclic changes, parasite load and rainfall, and (iii) the results of anti-helminthic drug treatment.

(e)   The idea of density dependence was covered in Box 4.1. Delayed density dependence refers to a situation where some density-dependent effect associated with an increase in grouse numbers (increased worm infection or increased aggressiveness) has an influence on population size (e.g. by increasing mortality) at a later time.

(f)   Overgrazing, improved upland drainage and increased aforestation are all mentioned as factors contributing to habitat decline. These factors all tend to reduce food and cover for the birds. Linked to this, conditions for predators (e.g. hen harriers) may have improved and habitat management is probably less intensive than before. The net result is that bird mortality increases at different points in the life cycle and fecundity may be reduced, e.g. due to reduced food for females.

(g)   No, this may indeed be the solution to the quandary. Contrasting points of view, expressed in the language of controversy, makes compelling reading, as here, but can sometimes obscure the fact that both interpretations are correct. There are a number of clues that grouse populations vary significantly—not all for example show the cyclic variation in numbers. With such a complex system, the interplay of the various factors (worms, behaviour and habitat loss) is likely to be intricate and to vary from one population to another.

(Incidentally, work after the conference reported here has implicated other factors in an increasingly complex picture—the contribution from a parasitic tick and the influence of a late spring, when birds hatch too late to take advantage of the abundant insect population in early June. Research findings in this field are usually reported in the popular press immediately prior to the onset of grouse shooting on the 'glorious 12th'.)

Activity 6.1

(a)   It is difficult to assess all of the article in detail, but quickly reading through the entire article should convince you that you can offer some insights into the contents of paragraphs 1 to 3. For example, biodiversity is defined in the article as 'everything that lives on the planet', i.e. it is taken to be equal to *global species richness*. Whilst this is a simplification—it is only one of the two elements of diversity used in the Simpson index—it is not inaccurate or grossly misleading; indeed biodiversity is often used as shorthand for 'species richness' (within a given area). Note that in paragraph 3 the upper limit for the total number of species is given as 80 million. This is very high compared with most estimates (see Section 2.2.1) and the word 'guess' is wisely used! Certainly the number of described species (about 2 or 3 million) is about right. So, the fact that the statements in paragraphs 1–3 agree broadly with what is known to be true can give us some faith that the other information in the article is accurate.

(b)   The extract states that the estimate for world species richness ignores 'microbes and fungi', essentially because they are small, difficult to sample, poorly described, and do not fall into conventional species categories.

Activity 6.2

(a)   There are a number of delays which slow down the process from data collection to publication. In this example, a major limiting factor was the enormous expert labour required for identification of the insects. Stork listed 35 taxonomists responsible for identifying the insects. (It is worth noting that an earlier related scientific paper was submitted for publication in 1987.)

(b)   Of course, a great range of responses is possible, but a 'flow-chart' approach such as Figure 6.5 is particularly helpful.

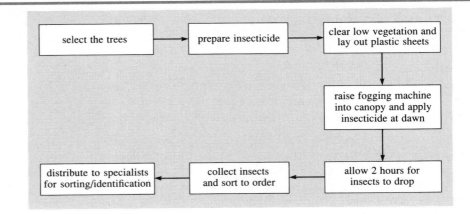

Figure 6.5 A possible answer to Activity 6.2b.

Activity 6.3

(a)(i)   To calculate the Simpson family diversity index, we use the number of species in each family as a proportion of the total number of species. For example, out of the total of 571 species 25 are found in the family Pselaphidae, i.e. a proportion of 25/571. If we sum $(25/571)^2 + (115/571)^2 \ldots + (129/571)^2$, we obtain 0.149. Subtracting this from 1 gives the Simpson diversity value of 0.851.

(ii)   The calculated value shows how evenly the species are spread amongst the ten families. It is difficult to assess the usefulness of this value as it is clearly a simplification of the data, but it can be used to get some feel for the beetle diversity in these trees without looking at the raw data.

(b)(i)   See Figure 6.6.

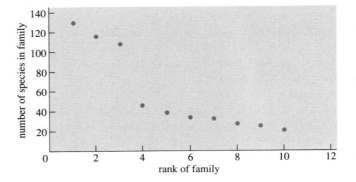

Figure 6.6 Rank–abundance curve for the number of species in ten Coleoptera families from ten trees in Brunei. Answer to Activity 6.3b.

(ii)   The graph shows that there are a large number of species in the three families with the highest number of species (all with more than 100 species) and that a sudden drop occurs between family 3 and 4. Whilst this information can be obtained from Table 6.4 it is easier to see from the graph. The graph therefore suggests an uneven distribution of species amongst families for the ten most abundant families.

(iii)   The other 50 families would form the 'tail' of the curve from family 11 through to 60.

(c)   The Simpson diversity index is highest when families contain equal proportions of species (or species contain equal proportions of individuals). This would produce a very flat rank–abundance curve. Although in our example the first three families have a high abundance of species, the remaining seven lie on a fairly 'flat' curve, resulting in the Simpson diversity index being quite high (0.85).

(d)   See Figure 6.7. Just plotting ten orders in this way should show strikingly that a very high proportion of the species are from the first five orders. The distribution of species amongst these insect orders seems much more uneven than for the distribution of species amongst beetle families (Figure 6.6).

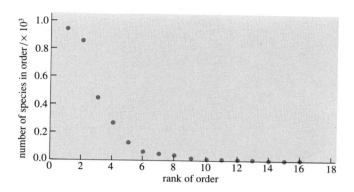

Figure 6.7   Rank–abundance curve for the number of species in the 16 insect orders from ten trees in Brunei. Answer to Activity 6.3d.

Activity 6.4

(a)   Of course there can be no right or wrong answer here. Compare your diagram with Figure 6.8. In what respects is it better/worse than your own? Decide how your approach (or mine!) could be improved.

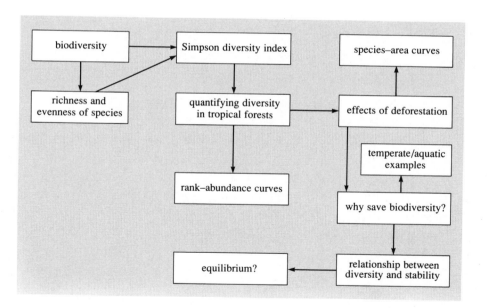

Figure 6.8   Sample answer to Activity 6.4a.

(b)   Figure 6.9 suggests possible approaches to Chapters 1–3. Our hope is that these will act as a sufficiently clear guide to enable you to tackle Chapters 4 and 5 entirely on your own!

You should have found the summaries of chapters useful to identify the key points. Once again, the layout of the diagram has to be largely your own choice but avoid too complex a style.

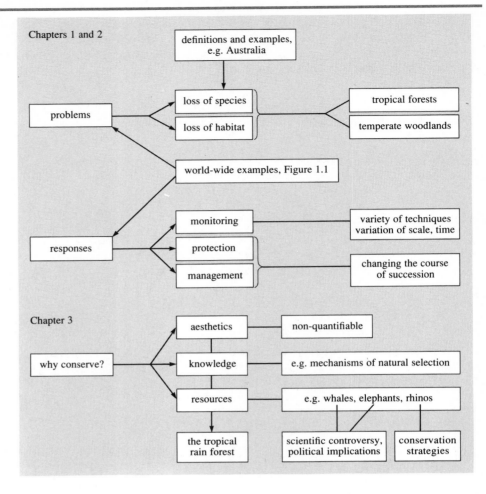

Figure 6.9 Sample answer to Activity 6.4b.

(c)   You may have thought of others for yourself, but Figure 6.9 identified the following, any two of which could provide the answer required.

(i)   Chapter 3 raises the 'why conserve' issue, which clearly has a bearing on 'why save biodiversity' in Chapter 6.

(ii)   Chapter 4 focuses on monitoring. Chapter 6 should have convinced you that this process is essential to any analysis of biodiversity—recall for example the work of Stork on insect species.

(iii)   Deforestation has been a major issue throughout the book—recall Extract 3.5 in Chapter 3; Chapter 6 considers this in relation to the effect of tropical deforestation on insect diversity.

(iv)   The concept of equilibria in populations was raised in Section 4.4.1 in the context of the size of populations, in a way that was relevant to Chapter 6, which considered the stability of ecosystems.

Acknowledgements

The Course Team would like to acknowledge the help and advice of the external assessor for this book, Dr M. J. Hutchings of University of Sussex, and the comments received from Dr N. E. Stork, British Museum (Natural History).

Grateful acknowledgement is made to the following sources for permission to reproduce material in this book:

Text

Extract 3.1 Concar, D. and Cole, M. (1992) 'Conservation and the ivory tower', *New Scientist,* 29 February 1992; *Extract 3.2* Hadfield, P. (1992) 'African nations defeated over elephant trade', *New Scientist,* 14 March 1992; *Extract 3.3* Pellew, R. (1992) ' "Hollow victory" of ivory trade ban', *The Times,* 23 March 1992, © Dr Robin Pellew; *Extract 3.4* Armstrong, S. (1989) ' "Nose" jobs save Namibian rhinos', *New Scientist,* 18 November 1989; *Extract 3.5* Fellows, L. (1992) 'What are the forests worth?', *The Lancet,* **339**, 30 May 1992, The Lancet Ltd; *Extract 4.1* Davies, G. (1986) 'The orang-utan in Sabah', *Oryx,* **20**, Blackwell Scientific Publications Ltd; Extracts 5.1, 5.3 Thomas, A.S. (1960) 'Changes in vegetation since the advent of myxomatosis', *Journal of Ecology,* **48**, Blackwell Scientific Publications Ltd; *Extract 5.2* Tittensor, A. (1983) 'Myxomatosis in decline?', *Country Life,* IPC Magazines Ltd, © Andrew Tittensor; *Extract 5.6* Reprinted by permission from *Nature,* **343**, pp. 310–311, © 1990 Macmillan Magazines Ltd; *Extract 6.1* Radford, T. (1992) 'Healing force of evolution', *The Guardian,* 6 June 1992; *Extract 6.2* Stork, N. E. (1991) 'The composition of the arthropod fauna of Bornean lowland rainforest trees', *Journal of Tropical Ecology,* **7**(2), May 1991, Cambridge University Press.

Figures

Figure 1.1 (1) Dayton, L. (1990) 'World's largest buffalo herd under threat', *New Scientist,* 15 September 1990; *Figure 1.1 (2)* 'Bleak future for British conservation', *New Scientist,* 1 December 1990; *Figure 1.1 (3)* 'Flushed sewers spell the end for Parisian fish', *New Scientist,* 14 July 1990; *Figure 1.1 (5)* ' "Cuddly" orang-utans threatened by traders', *New Scientist,* 8 December 1990; *Figure 1.1 (6)* 'Lethal capture', *New Scientist,* 15 September 1990; *Figure 1.1 (7)* 'Albatross fall for the bait', *New Scientist,* 29 September 1990; *Figure 1.2 (1)* 'A home fit for macaques', *New Scientist,* 21 July 1990; *Figure 1.2 (3)* 'East German police keep eagle eye on eggs', *New Scientist,* 4 August 1990; *Figure 1.2 (4)* 'Making a meal of extinction', *New Scientist,* 8 December 1990; *Figure 1.2 (5)* Glasgow, E. (1990) 'New Zealand declares war on the possum', *New Scientist,* 23 June 1990; *Figure 1.2 (7)* 'Kites flying', *New Scientist,* 21 July 1990; *Figure 1.2 (8)* 'Ranching of rarities angers ecologists', *New Scientist,* 20 October 1990; *Figure 1.2 (9)* Spinks, P. (1990) 'Replanted rainforest could "offset" Dutch coal-fired power stations', *New Scientist,* 21 April 1990; *Figure 1.2 (10)* 'Nuts to plastic buttons', *New Scientist,* 15 September 1990; *Figure 2.1* Ardea Ltd, London; *Figures 2.3, 2.4 a,c, 2.5* From *The Pictorial Atlas of Australia,* © 1977 George Philip Ltd; *Figure 2.6* Figure from Krebs, C. J. *Ecology,* © 1985 by Harper & Row, Publishers, Inc. Reprinted by permission of HarperCollins Publishers; *Figure 2.7* based upon Richards, P.W. (1981) *The Tropical Rain Forest,* Cambridge University Press; *Figures 2.8, 2.9* adapted from Hall, P. C. (1980) *Sussex Plant Atlas,* Booth Museum of Natural History, Brighton, Brighton

Borough Council; *Figure 2.10* Turner, C. (1970) *Philosophical Transactions of the Royal Society of London*, B, **257**, pp. 373–437; *Figure 3.1* Laws, R. M. (1962) 'Some effects of whaling on the southern stocks of baleen whales', The Exploitation of Natural Animal Populations, in Le Cren, E. D. and Holdgate, M. W. (eds) *Symposium of the British Ecological Society*, **2**, pp. 137–158, Blackwell Scientific Publications Ltd; *Figures 4.1, 4.2, 4.3* Hutchings, M. J. (1987) 'The population biology of the early spider orchid', *Journal of Ecology*, **75**, Blackwell Scientific Publications Ltd; *Figure 4.8a* Burton, J. A. and Pearson, B. (1987) *Collins Guide to Rare Mammals of the World*, Collins, an imprint of HarperCollins Limited; *Figure 4.8b* Frank Lane Picture Agency; *Figure 6.1* Illustration from Krebs, C. J. *Ecology* (2nd edn) © 1978 by Charles J. Krebs. Reprinted by permission of HarperCollins Publishers.

Table

Table 2.2 Grainger, A. (1983) 'Improving and monitoring of deforestation in the humid tropics', in Sutton, S. L., Whitmore, T. C. and Chadwick, A. C. (eds) *Tropical Rainforest: Ecology and Management,* Blackwell Scientific Publications Ltd.

Colour Plates

Plates 2,1a, b Science Photo Library, National Remote Sensing Centre; *Plate 2.2* James Bullock; *Plates 3.1a, 5.2a, 5.2b* Heather Angel Biofotos; *Plate 3.2* P. J. DeVries, Austin, Texas; *Plate 4.1* M. J. Hutchings.

Index

Note: Entries in **bold** are key terms. Page numbers in *italics* refer to figures and tables. Colour plate numbers are prefixed by 'Pl'.